Advance Praise for *Hit the Ground Running*

"I read *Hit the Ground Running* from cover to cover. It is a great read and one of the most interesting and useful business books I have ever read."
—Jim Goodnight, CEO, SAS Institute

"*Hit the Ground Running* proves that good guys can and do finish first when they provide value-centered leadership that places the needs of customers, employees, and shareholders before the needs— or ego—of the CEO. A great read for any aspiring leader."
—Kevin L. Robert, CEO, Wolters Kluwer Tax and Accounting

"*Hit the Ground Running* boils down the experience of ten successful new CEOs. The result is a list of rules any leader—new *or* seasoned—can live by."
—Mike Koehler, president and CEO, Teradata Corporation

"Jason has hit the mark again! The journey of each CEO reminds me of my favorite Bible verse about business, 'The reward of humility and the fear of the Lord are riches, honor, and life.'"
—Larry P. Ferguson, chairman and CEO, Schreiber Foods

HIT THE GROUND RUNNING

HIT THE GROUND
RUNNING

A MANUAL FOR NEW LEADERS

JASON JENNINGS

PORTFOLIO

PORTFOLIO

Published by the Penguin Group

Penguin Group (USA) Inc., 375 Hudson Street, New York, New York 10014, U.S.A.
Penguin Group (Canada), 90 Eglinton Avenue East, Suite 700, Toronto, Ontario,
Canada M4P 2Y3 (a division of Pearson Penguin Canada Inc.)
Penguin Books Ltd, 80 Strand, London WC2R 0RL, England
Penguin Ireland, 25 St. Stephen's Green, Dublin 2, Ireland (a division of Penguin Books Ltd)
Penguin Books Australia Ltd, 250 Camberwell Road, Camberwell, Victoria 3124, Australia
(a division of Pearson Australia Group Pty Ltd)
Penguin Books India Pvt Ltd, 11 Community Centre, Panchsheel Park,
New Delhi–110 017, India
Penguin Group (NZ), 67 Apollo Drive, Rosedale, North Shore 0632, New Zealand
(a division of Pearson New Zealand Ltd)
Penguin Books (South Africa) (Pty) Ltd, 24 Sturdee Avenue, Rosebank,
Johannesburg 2196, South Africa

Penguin Books Ltd, Registered Offices: 80 Strand, London WC2R 0RL, England

First published in 2009 by Portfolio, a member of Penguin Group (USA) Inc.

10 9 8 7 6 5 4 3 2 1

LIBRARY OF CONGRESS CATALOGING IN PUBLICATION DATA
Jennings, Jason.
  Hit the ground running : a manual for new leaders / by Jason Jennings.
     p. cm.
  Includes index.
  ISBN 978-1-59184-247-7
  1. Leadership.   2. Executive ability.   3. Success in business.   I. Title.
  HD57.7.J468 2009
  658.4'092—dc22   2008045302

Printed in the United States of America

This book is dedicated to
George Staubli

Contents

Contents

Introduction

Every manager or leader needs to *hit the ground running!*

When you're given the opportunity to take charge and you get it right, you put yourself on your leadership's radar. Do it right a second time and you'll become known as a *go-to* manager who can be trusted to deliver results.

But if you don't get it right, you'll join a long list of question marks at your company. Sure you may get another chance, if the "A" list is unavailable or nobody else wants the assignment. But fail to get it right a second time and you'll get yourself on that other executive radar system—the one that warns boards and bosses that they're making a risky bet when they choose you. Who's willing to hire, promote, take a chance on, and trust someone with a big question mark written on his back? (And who's motivated to work for him?)

The stakes for executives are now higher than ever. Movers are getting a lot less time to become shakers. On average, upper managers get just about three years to work their magic. Then they either move on or move out.

So whether you're starting a new career, launching a new product, or positioning yourself to take on bigger responsibilities, it's imperative that you know how to get up to speed, make good decisions quickly, and begin producing positive results fast.

The big question is, "What are the right steps to ensure that you will hit the ground running?"

You Need a Front-Row Seat

It would be great if organizations had a manual for their new leaders, a collection of dos and don'ts learned the hard way—through trial and error in the real world of day-to-day business at your company.

But I'll bet you've never seen one. Few of us have. Ninety-three percent of executives admit their company doesn't keep any reliable record of the steps that led to their best or worst management decisions. So there's little practical wisdom to follow. Memories are unreliable. People count their hits and routinely forget their misses. Academics may have interesting findings and insight, but their advice is generally not battle-tested. That leaves most of us condemned to make many of the same mistakes as previous generations and learn only from our own experiences as we go up the chain of command.

I recall an argument I had with my father when I was a teenager and being as obnoxious as only sixteen-year-old boys can be. Finally, in utter exasperation, my father looked at me and very calmly said, "Son, it's a wise man that learns from his experiences but a far wiser man who learns from the experiences of others as well." That's especially true if you want to hit the ground running.

The promise of this book is that you'll learn the tactics, strategies, values, and guiding principles of the best CEOs—each with a proven record of successfully taking charge and getting their companies on track to outperform all others. How much is that worth?

One of the CEOs in the book repeatedly expressed his gratitude for having had front-row seats twice during his career and being able to watch masterful CEOs do their job. Another was equally grateful for the time he spent seeing bad tactics lead to bad results. It gave him a great list of what *not* to do.

The things you'll learn in the following pages are the equivalent of you having those same front-row seats and watching and learning from the best in the world.

The Role Models

You're about to meet America's best performing CEOs.

They are the best CEOs in the nation because during the time period studied they created more economic value for their companies and shareholders than all the other CEOs of America's top one thousand companies.

Each CEO distinguished himself by quickly sizing up the situation, stopping any bleeding, seeing through the fog, selecting a destination, assembling the right team, building a strategy, and rapidly achieving great results. They all hit the ground running.

Our research travels took us from the industrial countryside of Georgia to specialty steel plants to office superstores. We hung out with natural gas exploration crews on the sun-blasted deserts of Utah, got stuck in New England blizzards, managed a sneak peak at futuristic aerospace technology, and played with the latest battlefield communications gear.

As we pored through the thousands of pages of transcripts trying to connect the dots we came to three realizations:

- All the CEOs we identified got their companies moving in the right direction really fast. They didn't wait for consultants to report or dawdle indecisively for an eternity before making the first move. Their instincts were terrific; they came prepared with outstanding new ideas and were able to get people pitching in immediately.

- Each CEO was guided by a set of rules for taking charge that challenges conventional thinking. They didn't automatically replace existing staff or bring in their cronies. They didn't put the fear of God into everyone. They didn't spin or make any "the ends justify the means" rationalizations. Their rules were very different from what we've been told are the practices of the hardest-charging, highest-performing CEOs.

- Most important, each CEO made everyone proud. What these new CEOs did and the way they went about it was right for investors, right for employees, right for their communities, right for the short run, and right for the long run. It made people proud and that created a lot of momentum.

Collectively these CEOs confronted every imaginable business challenge and problem, and we were blown away by their remarkable insights, their authenticity, their calm sense of peace and certainty, and their willingness to share everything they'd learned throughout their life and business journeys.

In short, these new leaders gave us what can fairly be called the golden rules for hitting the ground running.

Here's How We Found Them

We studied the performance of all the CEOs who'd taken charge of the thousand largest publicly traded companies in the United States. Collectively these companies generate more than $12 trillion in annual revenues and account for more than 80 percent of the total economic activity generated by all 11,000 public companies in the nation.

We didn't include any privately held companies because they're notorious for holding their financial cards close to their vests. We also didn't investigate any leader's performance prior to 2001 because the world has changed since the end of the twentieth century in so many ways, including the Sarbanes-Oxley Act, which requires the CEOs of all publicly traded companies to personally attest to the accuracy of their financial reporting.

There were three other standards in our search: The CEOs had to have been on the job for at least three years; the companies had to be clean; and the CEO had to still be on the job. It can sometimes take a few years to implement change and realize its full financial impact; we didn't want to write about companies that dump toxic waste in people's backyards; and, if the CEO had left the company, he'd probably be unwilling or unable to talk openly about his time in charge.

The best way to measure the performance of a CEO and compare one to another is to calculate the total amount of economic value they've created. We defined economic value as the sum of the profits generated, dividends paid, increases in sales and profits, and the increase in the company's share price during the CEO's tenure.

Between 2001 and 2007 the average *Fortune* 1000 CEO who'd been on the job at least three years and was still in the chair managed to increase his company's revenues by 55 percent, earnings per share by 68 percent, EBITDA (earnings before interest, taxes, depreciation, and amortization) by 164 percent and net profit margins by 5 percent.

The CEOs who made our cut include people who took over companies because of death, retirement, resignation, or the poor performance of their predecessor, and each far outperformed the average CEO performance. The CEOs we identified almost doubled revenues, more than tripled earnings per share, nearly tripled EBITDA, and doubled their company's net profit margins.

The Nation's Best Performing CEOs 2001–2007

- **Patrick Hassey** ended a streak of ten consecutive money-losing quarters after he took over troubled Allegheny Technologies. In the two years that followed, the company's revenues doubled and the company's share price increased 900 percent.

- **Marshall Larsen,** hugely influenced by his time at West Point and as a captain in the U.S. Army, has spent his entire career with BF Goodrich. He operates it with military precision and has led this former tire maker into becoming a world leader in aerospace systems as Goodrich Corporation.

- **Frederick Eppinger** had family members who'd spent more than forty years working for The Hanover Group, but by the time he took over most people were embarrassed to admit they worked for the company. During his first three years at the helm he doubled the firm's earnings per share, tripled its share price, and made everyone proud.

- **Howard Lance,** the first outside CEO in the history of the Harris Corporation, proved to be the exception to the fact that outsiders underperform. During his first three years as CEO, the company more than doubled its earnings per share and share price.

- **Jeffrey Lorberbaum** became the CEO of Mohawk Industries while it was still just a carpeting company. Through a rapid series of twenty successful acquisitions, this CEO has transformed the company into a totally integrated flooring company with a commanding market share.

- **Ronald Sargent** spent fifteen years serving in numerous capacities at Staples, the world's largest office products company, before taking over as CEO in 2002. With an emphasis on growing the top line, he's achieved routine double-digit revenue growth and annual revenues heading for $28 billion, and more than doubled both the company's stock price and earnings per share.

- **Keith Rattie,** a former long-haired, guitar-playing idealist, never dreamed he'd end up as the CEO of natural gas giant Questar. But since Rattie took the reins in 2002, the company has become a favorite of environmentalists while more than doubling its share price and tripling earnings per share.

- **Mike McCallister** is the CEO of Humana Inc. This $20 billion giant believes that health insurance is broken and is determined to replace a crippled, complex, and confusing system with one that works. The company has more than tripled revenues, earnings, and share price since this former hospital administrator took over as CEO.

- **Tim and Richard Smucker** also prove to be the exception to the fact that ninety-nine times out of one hundred, great-grandsons fail their family businesses. But since Tim and Richard took over as co-CEOs of The J. M. Smucker Company, they've created leading positions in eight cutthroat grocery categories and added billions in new business.

You're about to meet and get to know the CEOs who took over companies, hit the ground running, and did a better job of creating shareholder value than all their peers. As you read you'll learn a set of rules that, if followed, will guarantee your success and the achievement of your full economic potential. And you'll find the answers to every business question you'll ever have. This is the manifesto for doing things the right way.

Jason Jennings
Timber Rock Shore
October 2008

Do You Have What It Takes?
Twenty Quick Questions

This is a short, multiple choice quiz. You can't pass or fail and you won't get a grade. The questions are designed to be thought provoking and prepare you for the remarkable advice and guidance from America's best performing CEOs who you'll be reading about in the coming pages. The answers appear on page 13. No peeking.

1. You're in a dog-eat-dog business with lots of competition for every customer. You and your brain trust have just landed on a great new strategy for achieving your market share and revenue goals. Do you:

   a. Keep it under lock and key
   b. Share the strategy but only on a need-to-know basis
   c. Publish your strategy for everyone to see

2. Your company needs to significantly increase revenues. You have found a great candidate for sales manager and are convinced she could increase sales by 50 percent in her first year. The only potential problem is that she doesn't exactly share the company's values. Do you:

    a. Hire her because diversity of values is a good thing

    b. Hire her and hope she "comes around"

    c. Pass on this candidate and keep interviewing

3. You're a senior leader within an organization. You and your team have just completed a presentation you'll be making to the top bosses or board of directors. You should:

    a. Do the presentation yourself

    b. Have a more junior member of your team do it

    c. Do a joint presentation with you and your team

4. What's the best way to gain the belief of the people who work for you?

    a. Ask for their trust

    b. Take a workshop in building a personal leadership brand

    c. Just get on with it—they'll come around

5. You've just been appointed CEO. The company is in trouble. Do you:

    a. Replace most of the leadership team with people you've worked with previously and who you can count on for loyalty

    b. Keep much of the current leadership team in place

    c. Make your decision about who stays and who goes after you've been there six months

6. When starting a new leadership position should you:

    a. Have a strategy in place before you start the job

    b. Start building a strategy once you're on the job

    c. Continue implementing the strategy that's in place and take some time to analyze the results

7. Outright asking for the help of your bosses (including the board of directors if you're a CEO) will be seen by them and others as:

    a. Something you should readily do
    b. Something you'd hesitate to do

8. When someone moves into a management/leadership position, she generally achieves her highest level of performance during:

    a. Year 1
    b. Year 5
    c. Year 9

9. Most of America's top-performing CEOs:

    a. Grew up poor
    b. Grew up middle class
    c. Grew up well off

10. How much time does a leader have to make a bold symbolic gesture to a company's work force about the future direction of the enterprise?

    a. One hundred days
    b. Six months
    c. One year

11. What's the most frequently cited reason why workers leave companies?

a. They can earn more money elsewhere

b. They don't like the company's values

c. They don't like their boss

12. The most effective compensation program:

    a. Rewards people for the results they were asked to achieve

    b. Rewards people for the success or failure of the total company

    c. Rewards people for the success or failure of their team

13. How far out should an effective leader be able to see?

    a. Six months

    b. One year

    c. Five years

14. When you are in a leadership position within an organization you should:

    a. Share the limits of what you can or cannot approve

    b. Never reveal to others what you can or cannot approve

15. You're in charge of transforming an organization. You should do it:

    a. All at once—get it done, face the pain, and get through it

    b. One small bite-sized piece at a time

    c. Slowly so people can adjust

16. Most of America's best performing CEOs have a college degree in:

    a. Marketing

    b. Political science

    c. Finance

    d. Engineering

17. The number one cause of failure in American business is:

    a. Lack of working capital

    b. Competitive pricing

    c. Copying a competitor's strategy

18. Which assignment would best prepare you to become a top-performing CEO?

    a. Something significant in marketing or finance

    b. A turnaround of a small, money-losing operation

    c. A six-month stint on the executive strategy council

19. CEOs need to ask a lot of

    a. Smart, laser-focused questions

    b. Dumb, sometimes painfully naive questions

    c. Neither—the CEO should have the answers

20. The top trait of the best performing CEOs is

    a. Adaptability

    b. Assertiveness

    c. Authority

The correct answers: 1 (c), 2 (c), 3 (b), 4 (a), 5 (b), 6 (b), 7 (a), 8 (a), 9 (a), 10 (a), 11 (c), 12 (c), 13 (c), 14 (b), 15 (b), 16 (b), 17 (c), 18 (c), 19 (b), 20 (a)

Rule 1: Don't Deceive Yourself—You Will Reap What You Sow

Because Smucker's jams, jellies, and marmalades are household names and the company has been around for more than one hundred years, most people would be surprised to know that its current CEOs personify leaders who hit the ground running.

Since Tim and Richard Smucker, cochairs and co-CEOs, took charge of the company upon the death of their father, they've acquired thirteen companies, introduced an average of fifty new products each year, and increased revenues from $660 million to a projected $4.7 billion in 2009 (following their planned acquisition of Folgers coffee). If you want a case study in great leadership, you needn't look further than The J. M. Smucker Company.

I learned one of this book's most important lessons while sitting at a long conference table in the boardroom of The J. M. Smucker Company on Strawberry Lane in Orrville, Ohio. Tim and Richard Smucker said something that affected me deeply. "You have to remember," said Richard, "that our company was founded by a devout, God-fearing man, and *everything* he did was based on a single verse from the New Testament. Our great-grandfather, James Monroe Smucker, kept a board hanging above his desk for his entire working life that had a quote from Galatians, Chapter 6, Verse 7, that said: 'Be not deceived; God is not mocked: for whatsoever a man soweth, that shall he also reap.'"

I never missed Sunday school as a child and had learned the quote from Paul's letter to the Galatians that said, "As you sow, so shall you reap," but for some reason I'd missed the "do not be deceived, God is not mocked" part. That says loudly and clearly that there's no sense in trying to fool yourself, anyone else, or God. It's inescapable. Whatever a person sows, he'll reap the deserved results. You can't talk or scheme your way out of it. Don't be deceived!

"Think about the profound implications of that," interrupted Tim. "A natural extension of that basic belief is the Golden Rule which is stated in Matthew and other books of the Bible as: So *in everything*, do unto others as you would have them do unto you."

Following my interview, as I toured the ancestral home of J. M. Smucker and the state-of-the-art complex next door where the company makes nearly a million bottles of jam, jelly, and apple butter each day, I kept replaying all the earlier CEO interviews in my mind. The connection was obvious. It was one overpowering characteristic that all the CEOs shared: They told the truth. None of them deceived themselves about anything, nor did they surround themselves with executives who did; they all practice the Golden Rule; and, as a result, they've become the best performing CEOs in the nation.

The J. M. Smucker Company

Jerome Monroe Smucker, a dairy farmer and Mennonite, learned very early in life the importance of hard work when his mother died and he was put in charge of his younger brothers and sisters. While his father had shortened the family name Schmucker to Smoker, Jerome's deeply held religious beliefs couldn't tolerate being called a smoker so he changed it back to something more closely resembling the original Swiss-German.

Besides tending his dairy herd J.M. was also an educator and, according to family lore, a tinkerer always trying to figure things out. According to his great-grandsons Richard and Tim, J.M. pressed cider at a small mill he opened in 1897 using apples from trees that had been planted by Johnny Appleseed earlier that century. In one of the early acts of "lean" production, his tinkering led him to figure out a way to reduce the length of time it took to make apple butter from eight hours to a little more than two hours (increasing his productivity by a factor of four). He began selling the apple butter to neighbors. "He was," says Richard, "proud of his work and signed his name on the top of each crock as his personal guarantee."

It's possible that J.M.'s affinity for tinkering was genetically inspired and part of the family's DNA because it's a trait that's been strongly exhibited by each succeeding generation and in large measure, a key ingredient in the company's success.

By 1900 J.M.'s son Willard had joined his father and they expanded the family business by traveling and selling their apple butter from the back of a horse-drawn wagon. In the early 1920s the firm began bottling and selling the jams and jellies that have become a household name.

The early 1940s saw the first national distribution of Smucker's products with a shipment by train to Los Angeles. In 1959 the company went public with the family retaining voting control. Then, in 1962, the company made its first foray into national advertising when the legendary Wyse advertising agency coined a phrase most Americans recognize, "With a name like Smucker it has to be good."

The 1970s were breakthrough years for the company. In quick succession it introduced fruit syrups and peanut butter, completed its first major acquisition by buying a gourmet line of preserves and jellies, and after more than eighty years in business finally established market leadership for the first time. The 1980s and 1990s saw more acquisitions and the firm's first international expansion. In 1998 (and every year since) *Fortune* magazine named Smucker's one of the top one hundred companies to work for, and following its acquisition of Jif, Crisco, Pillsbury, and Folgers coffee, the company's brands currently hold leading positions in eight food categories.

There's an old Lancashire proverb about family-run businesses that says, "From clogs to clogs in only three generations." It implies that however successful a poor man may eventually make his business, his grandson or great-grandson will certainly wreck it, falling back to poverty and "clogs." Studies of American business prove that 99 percent of all family-controlled businesses disappear within one hundred years. Yet J. M. Smucker has weathered nineteen recessions and economic downturns and grown and prospered during four successive generations of family control. Since it went public, Smucker's stock has outperformed the S&P average stock by a factor of five.

Did J. M. Smucker simply accidentally stumble on the perfect bullet-proof business or are there greater forces at play?

"Dad made the decision that if we were going to be around for another hundred years we had to build our brands," Richard explains. "We felt that we had to become the leader. But [in everything] we take the long-term perspective. We might change tactics. But we won't change our ethics. The value system that was established by J. M. is the value system that we go by today."

"If you want to build a highly successful and enduring enterprise," Richard and Tim Smucker say, "you must practice the Golden Rule."

Tim and Richard Smucker

Former chief of the international grocery chain IGA and longtime observer of consumer goods businesses, Dr. Tom Haggai warned me, "The hardest thing to believe in writing the story of Tim and Richard is that it's like the stories we were told as children—the good guys finish first. And they are really good guys; they still act like they were raised to act and on the same values they were given."

Tim and Richard grew up in small town Orrville in the fifties and sixties. "It was pretty Ozzie and Harriet," says Richard. "Pretty typical." Tim adds, "We went to school, played sports and we weren't 'A' students. We worked in the plant during the summers, loading trucks and cleaning."

The family was close knit. Both parents were excellent role models. Their father Paul was of the World War II greatest generation. "Dad spent two years on a destroyer," Tim says. "Saw a lot of action, kamikazes flying at his ship . . . that kind of stuff. The service sort of defined him, you know. He went into the navy because it was the right thing to do.

"My father was also a visionary thinker," Tim says. He envisioned the global marketplace, the need for cutting-edge technology, and the value of making acquisitions. He also saw the potential for losing those things that truly made the Smucker Company special. In a letter left to be read after he was gone, Tim's dad shared four simple practices for managers that would make sure employees stayed motivated and proud to work for the company as times changed and the business expanded. "Say thank you for a job well done; listen with your full attention; look for the good in others; and have a sense of humor."

Their mother Lorraine was the matriarch of both the home and the business. "My mother was kind of a spiritual leader," Richard says, "who resolved conflicts and brought compassion, love, and caring." Her contribution was critical to the success of the company, according to experts who study family businesses. And her lessons affected both of her sons greatly. "Strength is fine but probably not as powerful as love and compassion," Tim says. "We need to express our female side much as we do our male side."

Both brothers got their college degrees and their MBAs, and then returned to Orrville to work in the family business. Tim focused on marketing and Richard on finance. "It allowed us to develop in different parts of the business," Tim says. And for ten years all three ran the company together.

"Dad let us do things that were outside his comfort level," Richard says. "We learned to recognize mistakes quickly and take action." Tim adds, "We also learned that unless you're stretching, going outside the envelope, you're not going to develop new ideas."

Today the brothers are equal in the chain of command as co-CEOs. "My father saw that we each had unique strengths that blended well together," Richard says. So he didn't see the need to name one son the sole CEO.

"It takes ego out of the equation," Richard adds. "And I think ego is a big reason why CEOs are successful or not."

"We worked by consensus long before it was fashionable," Tim says, explaining why they are able to make such an unconventional hierarchy work. "We worked in multifunctional task forces. That set the tone that we're all in this together as a team."

Here are the beliefs, values, and management practices that have allowed Smucker's to become one of the best-led companies in the world.

The Law of Reciprocity

"A natural extension of the basic belief that, *as you sow so shall you reap*," Tim told me, "is that if you put in a hard days work [focused on serving your customers] you will benefit from your labors."

It's known as the law of reciprocity, and business leaders routinely forget it's an irresistible force. Consider Sprint. It was forced to take a $29 billion write-down in large part because its good customers were defecting faster than its best marketing efforts could replace them. But despite the conventional wisdom, this disastrous client churn rate wasn't because of AT&T's deal for the new iPhone, the pricing of rival carriers, or any other uncontrollable events. The seeds of Sprint's unacceptable losses were planted months and years earlier when customers were left sorely disappointed with the services at Sprint. They were promised one thing and got less—and vowed to themselves that they'd switch cell phone providers as soon as they could. Sprint is reaping what it sowed.

Paul Smucker (Tim and Richard's father) was so concerned about customer disappointment that he asked every assembly line to add an extra measure of jelly or jam to every jar. "That's far better," Paul says, "than one person opening a jar and finding a half ounce less than they paid for."

That commitment continues today. I saw it firsthand as Smucker plant superintendent Bill Erickson showed me a unique quality control stop in his orange marmalade production line. We went up a flight of metal stairs, through a clean room door, and there was a running river of 175-degree marmalade illuminated from below. An eagle-eyed crew watched the flow for any bit of imperfect orange peel and scooped out all offenders. "When mom or grandma opens a jar of our marmalade we don't want them to be disappointed," Erickson said. He explained that the company had tried all the high-tech methods for scanning the product and found the careful eyes of real people focused on quality were still the best way to get this job done right. So that's what they do. And even more surprising was how Erickson and the staff in that steamy room were as motivated as Tim and Richard about making sure every ounce of their products made people smile.

"There are lots of people in business who preach these same values," observes Richard, "but at the same time they're preaching them they aren't living them. That's completely hollow. We don't do any preaching or public praying here, preferring instead to live our beliefs, let other people witness them in action, and hope they'll become ingrained in everything they do as well."

The Right Culture

A company has either the right culture that their leadership has worked relentlessly to move throughout the organization or the wrong one because the leadership couldn't be bothered with *soft* things like culture.

A simple test to determine a company's culture is to select a few people at random from within the organization and ask them to explain the company's culture. If the same or similar responses are heard from everyone and they explain the culture the leadership wanted to have in place, the company probably has the right culture. But if people gaze skyward looking for an answer or if widely dissimilar responses are heard, then a very different culture exists. It's a culture where everyone watches out for themselves and simply does their best to get by and survive.

Right cultures are big, bold, and aspirational, provide purpose, are ethical and inclusive; and feed people's souls.

Titled *Why We Are—Who We Are*, the culture of J. M. Smucker is described on posters, printed on almost every company communication, and taught in conference rooms at the company's Strawberry Lane headquarters. Everyone learns the culture and is invited to be an active member of the community.

The J. M. Smucker Company Culture

We are a culture of dotting the i's and crossing the t's, of doing things right and doing the right thing.

We are a culture of growth both individually and as a company.

Our culture is who we are and because of who we are.

Our commitment to each other, our customers and our consumers

(continued)

The J. M. Smucker Company Culture *(continued)*

As we look to a future of unlimited possibilities we recognize the principles that are instrumental to our success.

A culture deeply rooted in our basic beliefs, beliefs that are guideposts for decisions at every level.

We are a culture that encourages commitment to each other; clear communication and collaboration.

Vision.

A culture of appreciation, a family sense of sharing in a job well done and where every person can make a difference.

One example of J. M. Smucker's commitment to its culture is that people who don't believe in the culture don't fit in or work there.

Tim Smucker says, "It begins with the people we hire. We look for attitude before aptitude and character before credentials. We'll provide the training that will teach someone how to do a job but doing that for someone who doesn't want to be part of our culture would be foolish."

"For instance," says Richard, "if someone were capable of doubling our sales but didn't want to be part of our culture we wouldn't hire them. It would be too disruptive and damaging to what we've spent more than a century building."

"Now we don't say, 'Okay, this is our culture. Now we're going to tell you how to think.' The co-workers who join us and do the best here either come from a culture or have a strong desire to be a part of a team," says Tim.

When the company makes a mistake and hires someone who doesn't fit the company's culture, it takes quick and fair corrective action. "By the end of someone's first year it's obvious whether or not they're a fit for our culture," says Tim Smucker. "If they're struggling with a particular job but fit the culture we'll work with them to find another position where their talents can be better utilized. But if someone doesn't fit our culture, there's no point in going forward together and they leave."

Even though the company has been publicly traded for more than fifty years, Smucker's continues its efforts to make certain that even stock market analysts and the investment community understand the company culture. "We simply won't do anything only for the benefit of short-term performance," says Richard. "We do road shows, frequently host analysts here in Orrville, and are always happy to provide long-term guidance but they have to make their own financial forecasts. We'd never trade our culture for a few quarters of extraordinary financial performance.

"We have a policy," Richard says, "that we won't advertise on shows with violence, sex, bad language, or games of chance." It's a tough criterion for media buyers these days. Smucker's ad agency suggested that if it would relax those standards a little, it could get another 40 percent more bang for its buck. "We said no," Richard explains, adding, "in matters of style, swim with the current but in matters of principle, stand like a rock."

The culture of the J. M. Smucker organization also determines the way decisions are made. "Part of having a good culture," says Tim, "is making sure everyone is on the same page, shares the same destination, and then communicates that information throughout the company.

"Each month we get our key officers together for a half-day meeting to review key issues and business updates where decisions are made and future directions are determined," says Tim, adding, "in that respect we have more of a Japanese style of consensus management.

"When only the CEO makes decisions and announces them to the world like a divine revelation he'll have certain trouble ahead," says Tim, further explaining the company's cultural position on decision making. "Everybody walks into our meetings with an agenda and when we leave we make certain everyone is on the same page."

The brothers acknowledge that spirited discussion often takes place before an agreement is reached but when asked whether everyone leaves in complete agreement on everything, they respond by saying, "Generally, we're in complete agreement *before* the meeting begins. The answer to every decision is in our culture; it either fits or it doesn't."

Anyone attempting to be an effective leader without having the right culture is kidding himself and almost certainly doomed to fail. A basic need of human beings is to be part of something bigger or greater than themselves, have a sense of purpose, and have the promise of a better tomorrow. Having the right culture fulfills those needs.

Everyone Should Know the Strategy

Recently, I was hired to do a kick-off speech for one of America's largest insurance companies. My keynote to the company's top leaders was scheduled to follow the CEO's opening speech. I was particularly interested in hearing his remarks so I'd be able to emphasize some of his points in my own speech.

I showed up early, shook a lot of hands, and followed as everyone began making their way into the hotel ballroom. Suddenly, someone grabbed me by the arm and whispered, "Mr. Jennings, you'll have to wait out here while the CEO speaks," she said, "someone will come and get you when he's finished."

"What are you talking about?" I asked. "I know your CEO, we've talked about my speech and his, and he's expecting me to be in there."

"That's not possible," she said, as she led me away from the doors, "he might mention part of our strategy during his speech and no one outside the company is allowed to hear it unless they've signed a nondisclosure agreement." So I stood guarded in the hallway, silently fuming and feeling like a fifth wheel while this poor soul who was probably just following orders tried her best to make nice-nice.

Strategy isn't guarded with the same misplaced zealousness at Smucker's. Within minutes of the start of our first interview Richard Smucker said, "If you want to properly understand our company you need to know that everything begins with our values and that they are the foundation for and support our strategy."

I must have looked a bit puzzled because Tim Smucker said, "Here," pushing a book across the table, "this is our strategy."

Titled *Smucker's Corporate Strategy,* the small booklet contained the company's history, a description of the culture, and in easy-to-read and understandable language a recitation of the company's beliefs, its vision statement, core competencies, strategic architecture, size and growth, a scorecard, and a discussion of the strategic issues.

I asked if it would be possible to borrow a copy of the booklet during the book project and offered to sign a nondisclosure agreement if required. The brothers looked at each other, then at me, and laughed, and Tim said, "What kind of people do you usually hang around with? Of course you can have a copy. So can anyone else who wants one."

By correct definition a strategy is the BIG objective accompanied by the guiding principles that will determine how to achieve the objective. Any organization that's committed to the achievement of a BIG objective must work relentlessly to make certain everyone in the organization knows the strategy and believes they're playing a vital role in its achievement.

Secret Strategies Don't Work

People with secret strategies believe there are two classes of people—
those who need to know and those who don't. That's one big reason
most employees say they aren't sure they support their company's
strategy. They can't see the connection between the work they do and
their company's objectives. Inevitably, down the road, those same
executives with the right to know end up wringing their collective
hands in exasperation wondering why everybody else doesn't *get it.*

Here's what's wrong with secret strategies:

- **Secret strategies cause workers to become detached and
  disengaged.** A fall 2007 Gallup poll of the American workplace showed that 72 percent of American workers aren't
  engaged in their jobs. That's because they don't know why
  they're doing their jobs or what role they play in the company's ambitions. It isn't credible to ask people to contribute to the greater good when they don't know what the
  greater good is.

- **Secret strategies open the door for corners to be cut and
  unsavory (and maybe illegal) tactics to be employed.** The
  pressure to perform is unrelenting in today's business. In
  the interest of achieving short-term objectives, companies
  often resort to employing tactics that wouldn't be used if
  everyone knew the strategy. If everyone knows the strategy
  and somebody tries to do the wrong thing, there'll be a lot
  of wagging fingers pointing at them, saying, "No way!"

- **Secret strategies don't offer any accountability.** If everyone knows and embraces a strategy and it fails, then the
  people who led the effort failed. Keeping the strategy secret

26

means that fewer people will know of any failure and the strategic *geniuses* who created it might get to keep their jobs and perks.

Doubt Your Own Infallibility

Too frequently simply having an aura of power has been responsible for people landing in the CEO's chair. These are the imperial CEOs who are larger than life and frequently superficial. People see a lot more than they're given credit for and instinctively know whether or not someone is genuine. To be most effective, an authentic leader has to be willing remove the veneer and allow for his *fallibility*.

Tim and Richard Smucker bought Mrs. Smith's Pies and, in two short years, recognized "it wasn't going to be a good long-term fit." Infallible executives typically hold on to their mistakes, pouring good money after bad, until a failure becomes a disaster. But Tim and Richard sold Mrs. Smith's quickly for just a slight loss. "If we'd have held it for another three years," Richard explains, "we might have taken a large loss."

Contrast the Smuckers' willingness to admit they'd made a mistake with Carly Fiorina, former CEO of Hewlett Packard, who, despite not knowing the industry or the company, announced on her first day on the job that her strategy was set and then defended it throughout her entire agonizing reign. And even though reams of information had been proving for years that Vioxx was killing patients who used it, the company's former CEO refused to acknowledge the data; it would have made him fallible.

Tim Smucker quotes Benjamin Franklin, one of the nation's founders, who said in a letter and speech to the founding constitutional convention, "Doubt your own infallibility." "If you add a willingness to listen and a sense of humility to the ability to doubt your own infallibility you'll do well," says Smucker.

Don't Be Content

All businesses are going either forward or backward. There's never been a business in recorded history that achieved a utopian state and remained the same. Without growth a company will eventually be unable to hire and keep talented people. People work for businesses in the hope of achieving their own full economic potential. When highly talented and ambitious people discover that a brighter tomorrow doesn't exist, they'll leave at the first opportunity. Eventually the only people left will be those incapable of finding work elsewhere.

When questioned about their company's future growth prospects, Richard and Tim Smucker exchange smiles and say, "What we do is fun. The products we make put smiles on people's faces," asking rhetorically, "why would we ever want to stop doing that?"

"We'll be close to almost being a five billion following the acquisition of Folgers coffee," says Richard, and asks, "Why shouldn't we double or triple that?"

Don't Follow the Easy Money

Richard Smucker says that probably two thirds of his MBA graduating class was headed to Wall Street. "That's where the immediate money is. Lots of people worship money and celebrity and that's simply the wrong motive." He says, "We believe that a financial reward should be the by-product of doing something good."

Tim adds, "Size, growth, and profit are important . . . but they aren't the key drivers. We think that if we put the other things first (their values and their commitment to all the stakeholders), sales and earning will follow."

"We believe we have six constituents," Richard explains, "the consumer, the retailer, our employees, our suppliers, our communities, and our shareholders. Basically if we take care of those [first five], the sixth will automatically be taken care of. It's backwards from much of the Wall Street view."

The Smuckers' view was echoed by every CEO we identified and studied. Collectively, they argue that profit is not the reason for the existence of a company and that profit is a well-deserved by-product of doing what's right—and if they really do what's right, the profit will be there. They concur in the belief that if you're looking for more profit, the challenge is to do more good things.

That doesn't mean that The J. M. Smucker Company fails to make use of all the modern tools of production, marketing, logistics, finance, and so on. "In fact," Richard says proudly, "I'd put our people up against any in our industry. Nor does it mean [we] avoid making the tough decisions such as closing and consolidating inefficient plans, which we have done. But it's not only what you do but how you do it that counts."

Have Faith

Richard and Tim Smucker are devout members of the First Church of Christ, Scientist, commonly referred to as Christian Scientists. The brothers build a case for faith by saying, "We don't proselytize about our religion to others in the workplace but we actively encourage and hope that people will believe in *something*."

"We really respect everybody's individual independence and their right to believe in whatever they want," Tim explains. "When we talk about the Golden Rule, if you look at the Golden Rule in ten different beliefs, basically it's the same."

Interestingly, all the CEOs we identified are people of faith and could make up their own ecumenical council representing the Mormon, Catholic, Christian Science, Jewish, Presbyterian, Episcopalian, Lutheran, and Methodist faiths. Each CEO has a belief in something greater than themselves as individuals, and they all actively practice their faith.

Don't Be Deceived

When leaders and companies believe they're exempt from following the Golden Rule (like the greedy people who issued millions of bad mortgages and have nearly tanked the economic system of the United States), they inevitably end up deceiving others (workers, vendors, shareholders, suppliers, and customers) and deceive themselves into believing they'll get away with it. But they don't. Eventually karma prevails, their deceptions are revealed, they desperately try to clean up the messes they created, and they fail—all as a result of deceiving themselves and thinking *they* were exempt from following the Golden Rule.

When leaders or managers pronounce their workers the company's most important asset and then lay them off in order to hit the current quarter's numbers and earn their bonuses, they are deceiving themselves and they will have huge problems to fix. Their work force will become disengaged and untrusting, and years of tribal knowledge will be lost.

When they promise a customer everything to get them to buy and then deliver nothing without any option for fixing it, they're deceiving themselves, and they will face mass defections of customers. Trying to replace them will take all their time.

When they spin or fudge the numbers in an attempt to pump their share price in the short term, they're deceiving themselves and there will be retribution from lenders, class action lawsuits, and the SEC, which will keep their eyes off the ball and maybe land them in jail.

The shared values lived by the CEOs we studied are like a breath of fresh air in a world where deception abounds. Because so many high-profile companies (with few notable exceptions) have gotten away with lying to customers, shareholders, vendors, and employees with seeming impunity for years, we've come perilously close to having created a business culture where deceit is merely another tactic in the arsenal.

The words that appear in this chapter's title, "Don't Be Deceived," require little further explanation, and The J. M. Smucker Company is a great role model. Dr. Tom Haggai summed up my thoughts when he said, "I have greater confidence going forward with The J. M. Smucker Company than so many of the companies that are written about for one reason: They do what they say!"

Hit the Ground Running Rule 1
Don't Deceive Yourself—You Will Reap What You Sow

Tim and Richard Smucker's rules for achieving success in business include:

- Let the Golden Rule guide every decision.
- Don't have secret strategies—make sure everyone knows the strategy and knows their role.
- Have a culture that promises people a better tomorrow based on their good work.
- Don't be content; you're responsible for making things better.
- Doubt your own infallibility.
- Have faith. Believe in a higher force.
- Don't do what you know only for material rewards. Be called to your life's work and have a purpose.
- Laugh and have a sense of humor.

Rule 2: Gain Belief

Fred Eppinger knew The Hanover Group was in trouble when he accepted the role of CEO. The company had deep financial problems, the board wanted to see positive change, and the clock was ticking. Eppinger woke up very early to begin his first day on the job.

"I got to work about 6:00 A.M.," he says, "and the only way into the building at that time was through the back door of the cafeteria. As I walked through the kitchen I said to one of the staff, 'As long as you've got coffee brewing, may I have a cup?' She looked me up and down and said, 'Fine, but who are you?'"

"I told her I'd just been hired, that it was my first day, and that I wanted to get an early start and make a good impression."

As she reached for the carafe of fresh coffee, the woman asked what job he'd been hired to do. When he said that he was the new CEO, she almost dropped the pot. "I've been here fourteen years," she exclaimed, "and we've never seen any of the big-wigs down here before!"

Eppinger's next question must have been just as shocking. He asked if she'd mind sitting down and spending some time telling him about the company. It was the beginning of Eppinger's most important mission. He was going to enlist his employees, one person at a time, in turning around the company. Step one . . . gain belief.

The Hanover Insurance Group

The Hanover Insurance Group was formed more than 150 years ago in New York City to protect businesses and homeowners against the too frequent peril of fire. The company prospered and by early in the twentieth century was also insuring boats and automobiles. Because the company kept its assets largely liquid, it was able to survive the stock market crash of 1929 and the depression that followed. In 1969 the company relocated to Worcester, Massachusetts, in search of lower operating costs and a decade later was far outperforming the industry.

Postmortems of failed businesses almost always reveal that the seeds of their destruction were sown when the business appeared to be at its most robust. That was certainly the case with The Hanover.

"By the early nineties the company was already in trouble but didn't know it," says Eppinger. "A lot of mutually owned insurance companies during that time were headed by well-intentioned, albeit unsophisticated, investors whose hearts were in the right place but whose investment acumen wasn't up to snuff. People enjoyed working for them," he says. "They were great for their communities and it appeared their companies were growing but their core businesses just kept getting worse off.

"It was a different era," says Eppinger, clearly not wanting to judge too harshly. "We were supposed to be an insurance company but the place was really a big club. We owned a television station, produced the Bozo the Clown television program in our learning center, had a bowling alley, beauty and barber shops, were a big investor in McDonald's, and even owned the name Listerine," says Eppinger, wondering aloud why an insurance company would own the name of a mouthwash.

In the early nineties, following the deaths of two CEOs, the board acknowledged it needed to go outside the company for their next leader and chose someone who'd spent twenty years as an executive with Fidelity Investments in Boston. When the exec became CEO, the company consisted of two distinct businesses—life insurance and property and casualty insurance.

"The big problem," says Eppinger, "was that the new CEO, who'd been passed over for a top job at Fidelity, wasn't into the insurance business and set out to transform the company into an investment company that he hoped would rival his former employer Fidelity."

The company's traditional insurance businesses began cratering because it stopped using the cash it generated to fund its growth. Eppinger says, "He [that CEO] didn't pay it much heed because his chosen growth engine was going to be the variable annuity life business." Eppinger says the product was an annuity that provided the buyer a guaranteed periodic payout and a guaranteed death benefit.

"It took off like a rocket," says Eppinger, "but both the product and the way it was sold were seriously flawed. First, the company overpaid commissions in order to gain fast growth, then it assumed that stock markets would keep going up forever and they didn't bother reinsuring the policies because that would have depressed their earnings and operating cash."

For a while it appeared that Eppinger's predecessor might actually pull it off and create something he'd be able to merge with another company in hopes of becoming the joint CEO, thus thumbing his nose at his former Fidelity bosses. In 1995 he took the company public, changing the name to Allmerica. "Nobody who worked here could even spell the name Allmerica," says Eppinger, adding, "When I took the job my mother couldn't even pronounce it. She kept calling it All-America.

"The company became red hot," says Eppinger, "selling over 17 billion in annuities over a four- or five-year period, the company's stock price was soaring, reaching almost $70 a share, and the company was in merger talks when everything started to unravel. Older people were buying the annuities," he says, "because they were the customers attracted to the promise of the product," adding what actuaries have known for years: Old people die first and the death benefit has to pay off. During that CEO's entire tenure the company's chief actuary was never asked to give a report to the board of directors. "Then, the stock market dived," says Eppinger, "and he was in really big trouble, having forgotten the most important rule in the insurance business. You need reserves to cover your liabilities."

In 2002, a significant, sustained decline in the stock market—at the time, the worst since the Great Depression—placed an incredible strain on the life insurance company's capital and surplus position, prompting the major rating agencies to lower the company's financial strength ratings, which forced a decision to stop selling annuities and life insurance. Prior to this, the company was writing almost $4 billion annually of life insurance and annuity products. At the end of the year—zero.

Those circumstances led to the resignation of the company's chief executive officer, the elimination of hundreds of positions, and a dramatic decline in the company's stock price (the stock, which was over $67 per share the year before, dropped to $7.16 per share and investment banks were still shorting the stock). A dark cloud loomed over the company.

Over the next year, an interim management team comprised of the company's board chairman and three senior executives led a successful effort to stabilize the company's financial position, but the organization was adrift, without momentum or a captain to chart its course.

Enter Fred Eppinger.

Fred Eppinger

Eppinger grew up only twenty miles from The Hanover's impressive gray stone headquarters in Worchester, Massachusetts, and has had a lifelong familiarity with the company. "My uncle Frank worked for Hanover for forty-five years," he says, "my aunt Theresa was in the accounting department for thirty-five years, and my sister-in-law worked here for more than twenty. I remember as a kid being allowed to tag along to the annual Christmas party with my uncle Frank because I was the only other person in the family with a tie."

Soon after being hired as CEO Eppinger received a handwritten letter from his Aunt Theresa. It congratulated him on having become head of a company that had meant so much to her over the years but also contained a stern warning. "I have a pension," she wrote, "don't mess up."

In fact, The Hanover Group was more "messed up" and in bigger trouble than anyone at the company or even on the board of directors knew, and it would take every skill Eppinger had gained during his years in the industry to fix it.

Eppinger grew up as one of six children of fascinating parents. Because of the Depression, neither of his parents attended college, although both had been accepted to prestigious universities. "My parents are the most fiercely determined people I've ever met in my life and, at the same time, the nicest and most compassionate people you'll ever meet," Eppinger says.

The family turned to farming, and when asked about what cash crops they raised, Eppinger laughs. "We sold whatever moved— mostly chickens—and whatever didn't move including trees for lumber and rock from our own gravel pit. Our big business was chickens though. At any time we probably had three farms raising 30,000 to 50,000 chickens for us and three days a week we'd butcher three hundred a day and spend the other three days delivering them."

The family extracted a simple, but solid living from land they owned in rural central Massachusetts. "If the hay crop was good you'd get a few new pieces of clothing for school and if it wasn't you'd wear hand-me-downs," Eppinger says.

Eppinger was imbued with a strong work ethic. Eppinger's father, now in his nineties, remains active, running his own small business, painting, doing lawn work, and tending other peoples' properties. His mother, too, remains very active well into her eighties. Eppinger says that as a young man, his greatest desire was to be a farmer but that his father wouldn't hear of it. "My dad sat me down and said, 'Fred, you can always run a farm but I want you to have a choice to run a farm instead of *having* to run a farm—so you have to get an education.'"

Acquiescing to his father's wishes, Eppinger enrolled at the College of the Holy Cross in Worcester, Massachusetts, where he studied economics and accounting. "I worked as a tax preparer twenty hours per week during my four years in college," Eppinger says, "plus received a little money from home." His parents had accumulated enough farmland so that each year they would sell a few more acres to help pay for their children's college tuition, room, and board. "By the time I was a sophomore with a couple of years to go and a brother behind me who still had to go to school, they were down to only nine acres left," he says.

Following his graduation from Holy Cross, Eppinger joined Coopers & Lybrand, where, he says, "I knew almost immediately after starting as an accountant that I didn't want to spend my working lifetime recording another company's history in a ledger," adding, "I was probably the worst public accountant on the planet." Within two years he found himself back in school studying for an MBA at the Tuck School of Business at Dartmouth University.

One of Eppinger's professors at Tuck suggested that he join the consulting firm of McKinsey & Company. Eppinger imagined that his work at McKinsey would be only a short-term stop in his career. "I always thought I'd stay with them for two years, make some money, go home, and buy a business with my father," he says. But during his planned two-year stay something completely unexpected happened.

"I absolutely fell in love with the meritocracy of the place," he says. "It turned out it wasn't what I thought it would be," adding, "there were people from eighty countries, all different backgrounds, and it didn't matter who you were, what color you were, or what you looked like. All these people got thrown in a pile and great stuff happened. The only thing that mattered was achieving the result and doing great work.

"They sent me to see someone named Pete Walker who headed the firm's insurance practice," he says. "Pete was a consultant who truly loved getting into the grit and dirt of the turnarounds he helped to engineer." Eppinger joined the insurance practice and fifteen years later had become the person the firm called the *human white flag,* the go-to guy for turnarounds in the industry. Given that the insurance industry is highly regulated and full of buttoned-down conservative thinking, it was surprising to learn that turnarounds are frequently required.

"The volume of turnarounds required in the insurance business is because insurance companies do stupid things," says Eppinger in his characteristic straight-talk manner. "It's even worse than other businesses because insurance companies never know the true cost of their product for years until someone dies, has an accident, or a freak of nature causes mass destruction. Add to that the fact that insurance companies tend to be very bureaucratic entities that actively encourage people to *not* deliver the bad news and it's inevitable that blow-ups happen."

According to Eppinger, there are two main challenges in the insurance business that often cause companies to struggle or fail. "To begin with, insurance is a low-margin business (averaging about 5 percent) and it's hard to grow without adding new lines of business. The mistake some companies make is to expand into new lines before they have really done their homework, and before they make the necessary investments and build the capabilities to support their new product—and the result nearly always is a nightmare for those companies.

"Also," Eppinger says, "too many companies underwrite business and risks they don't fully understand, leaving the company and its customers dangerously exposed. It's a real recipe for disaster."

One example cited by Eppinger is an insurance company that decided to specialize in insuring gas stations, grew their business rapidly, but failed to do sufficient due diligence regarding buried gas tanks. When an epidemic of underground leaks occurred, the company ended up with a billion-dollar liability on its hands virtually *overnight*.

"Boom, gone," says Eppinger, "happens all the time." And nobody in the industry is exempt from making stupid mistakes. Citing the case of the world's second oldest insurance company, he says, "They decided to grow fast and to fuel that growth gave away their selling and underwriting pens to distributors who lied to them and wrote all kinds of shady business for them, which eventually blew up."

Ironically, the last insurance company that Eppinger ever thought would come close to going upside down was The Hanover Group. During his career at McKinsey, he and several other consultants had even written and published an article titled "The Journey" about the shared traits of truly great companies and one of the companies profiled was The Hanover Group.

By the time Eppinger arrived, the near total destruction was evident everywhere. "There was nothing good left when I arrived," he says. "The pension and life businesses weren't making any money, there was a broker dealer unit with seven hundred employees that was losing $70 million a year, the property and casualty business had shrunk ten years in a row and was only returning 3 percent, the billion-dollar annuity liability had become a $2 billion ticking time bomb. And to top things off, A. M. Best, an independent company that rates the financial strength of insurance companies, had downgraded the property and casualty company because of what it dubbed 'the contagion risk' of its association with the troubled life insurance business."

Conventional business wisdom dictated that the new CEO at Hanover would make a gallant entrance, whip out a sword, begin slashing jobs, and sell off pieces and parts to generate cash. That's not what Eppinger did. While he did make the difficult strategic decision to sell the company's life and annuity business, which would continue to operate as a run-off business, he began pouring energy, investment, and resources into restoring the strength and capabilities of the property and casualty business and making certain everyone knew their jobs were secure.

"I needed to quickly figure out what businesses we were in and who I could trust," Eppinger says. "But first I had to gain the belief and trust of the people who worked for the company so we'd have time to fix it." Immediately upon taking over Eppinger took the following steps.

He Got Rid of the Trappings

"After my conversation with the cook that first day," he says, "I headed up to my [new] office to check it out. Remember, I hadn't been in the building in the ten years since I'd written that article about the company. I couldn't believe my eyes. The previous CEO's office was unbelievable. There were massive sofas and chairs all over the place and a huge bar for his personal use.

"I took one look," Eppinger says, "and knew I couldn't possibly work there." He immediately called the building staff and asked if it would be possible to get him a computer and a light fixture so that he could work out of a cubicle in the reception area until they had time to remove the bar and fancy furniture from the office.

Out went the overflowing vases of flowers, the CEO's private elevator, the round-the-clock chauffeurs, and all the trappings of the royal CEO. "The Hanover's suite of executive offices, which previously was off limits for most employees, very quickly became an open, accessible and a very busy working space for a virtually nonstop schedule of roll-up-your sleeves meetings," Eppinger explains. "I put a whiteboard in my office and a conference table instead of a couch, so everyone knew that we were here to work and solve problems.

"Opening up the executive offices was more than just a symbolic gesture. It helped to announce a more open and accessible approach to management, but it also made a very clear statement about the shared responsibility and accountability among managers and leadership for solving our problems and setting a new course for the company. We were not going to be about the trappings of executive privilege. We were going to be about getting the job done and building something special together."

He Met with Everyone

As is common practice when a new CEO arrives, the chairman of the board took Eppinger around the headquarters building in Worcester and introduced him to key people. But Eppinger took a more unusual step and immediately began meeting with the two thousand workers in Massachusetts and the one thousand in Michigan in groups of fifty at a time.

"The meetings were heartbreaking in some ways," he says. "By the time I came on board half of the company's top three hundred executives had already left," adding, as an afterthought, "it's easy to understand why people didn't want to be here."

"The word 'embarrassed' came up a lot in those meetings," he says. "One person told me she'd been at a Christmas party, someone asked her where she worked and she said she was too embarrassed to say Allmerica."

"People were only here for a job," he says, "because they were paid decently and because there were good benefits. They weren't here for any higher purpose. That was the fire I had to rekindle."

He Asked for Their Belief in Him

One of Fred Eppinger's challenges was that while he was assessing the organization and coming to terms with the economic realities confronting him, he had nothing specific to tell or promise people about the company. But realizing that all people hope their tomorrow will be better than their today, he made certain promises.

"I told everyone quite bluntly," Eppinger says, "that I'm not stupid, that I came here for a reason and it wasn't to fail. The reason is because this was a great company once and we're going to make it great again."

Eppinger had gone back and studied the things he believed had originally made Hanover great and determined that it was financial strength, customer retention, development of people, a focus on execution, a strategy of partnering with agents, a host of innovative products, and responsive services.

"I told everyone that we don't have an absolute right to exist," he says, "that there were hundreds and hundreds of insurance companies and the world doesn't really need each and every one of them—but if we do the right things so that we deliver distinctive value to the market, then we can and will be a great company again." He promised he wasn't planning on selling the company and proposed the following deal to everyone. He asked employees to give up their cynicism and give him the benefit of the doubt during those first hundred days.

Eppinger threw down the gauntlet and challenged the company's employees. "I told our people that we were not going to focus on past mistakes. That from now on, we all needed to focus on fixing things and getting it right. And, with this in mind, we didn't need any intrigue or gossip around the water fountain," Eppinger says. "I don't need you to be the best of friends, but I do need—and frankly I expect—you to be respectful and professional colleagues. From now on, it's about working together to build a world-class organization. So, if you're up for the challenge, let's get to work. And if you're not, please leave today."

He made one more promise to everyone. "I told them they'd never be embarrassed again, this company would once again be a source of pride to all of its employees and to its home community." To demonstrate his commitment, Eppinger announced that the company would immediately double its contribution to its charitable foundation and begin giving back to the community where its employees live, work, and send their children to school.

When people asked how him how the company could afford to give money to the foundation, Eppinger responded, "We can't wait to act like a world-class company, we're going to start acting like a world class company right now and act that way every minute of every day."

Gaining Belief and Trust

Research shows that most people won't pitch in at the start of any change effort. Eighty-three percent prefer to sit on their hands. Why? They don't trust and they don't believe.

Until people trust, the manager leading them will be doubted and second-guessed, and the tactics he or she chooses to get to the destination will be questioned by way of rolled eyes, office gossip, and cynical suspicion. In many companies more time is spent on palace intrigue than on getting the job done because the workers don't buy into the goals, plans, ambitions, and promises of leadership.

There are four vital steps that need to be taken in order to gain the belief of your people, and the way Fred Eppinger went about it is a classic textbook example.

Make Your First Impression Great

Countless studies have assessed the impact of first impressions, and most conclude that within the first minute or less (one hundred milliseconds in one Princeton study) people have judged your education and economic levels as well as your authenticity. Within only a few minutes they've judged your intelligence, likeability, enthusiasm, confidence, competence, and compassion.

Studies have also shown that these instant impressions are incredibly stubborn, lasting a very long time and influencing how people feel about you despite contradictory evidence that shows up later. Experts confirm that old adage is true: You can't overestimate the power of the first impression.

When Pat Hassey took over as CEO at Allegheny Technologies, the company was in trouble and the workers were hoping that an improving economy could rescue them. During his first day on the job as employees welcomed him, he asked them to call him Pat. And during the weeks and months that followed his greeting remained the same. "I'm Pat," he'd say, "and I'm glad *you're* here." Hassey is on record as saying, "People never quit a company; they quit a boss," adding, "if people don't believe you they'll leave as soon as it's convenient for them to do so."

One can only imagine the impact of Fred Eppinger humbly introducing himself to a worker in the cafeteria and asking her to tell him about the company. How long do you think it took for that exchange to be communicated to the thousands of people throughout headquarters?

If authenticity, confidence, humility, and enthusiasm are missing in a leader's introduction, he's DOA.

Demonstrate a Point of Difference

A study taken of the American workplace in the fall of 2007 by the Gallup polling organization found that more than 70 percent of workers in America say they're not engaged in their jobs. Is the fact that most workers simply show up and put in their time a commentary on the work ethic of the American worker or does it make a bigger statement about a lack of inspiring leadership?

After months of witnessing the cratering of the company and the mass defection of co-workers, one can only imagine the impact of Fred Eppinger's carefully chosen words (one of his outstanding points of difference). "I told everyone that I did not come to this company to fail. I came here because this was a great company once and we're going to make it great again."

Like Eppinger, Pat Hassey at Allegheny has little use for regal surroundings, and like the disdain Eppinger demonstrated for working in his predecessor's nightclub-like office, he immediately closed the previous CEO's private bathroom, cut the office size in half, and let the word spread. "I needed people to believe and trust me," he says, "and that doesn't happen if you're being called Mister and isolated in a royal suite of offices."

Even though Ron Sargent had already spent twenty years at Staples and was already the number two person in the company when he was named CEO, he also felt compelled to demonstrate his point of difference so that his co-workers would believe in him. He spent his first day as CEO wearing a red uniform and working in a store waiting on customers and abiding by the same rule as every other corporate staffer: When you're in a store, you greet every co-worker by name and every customer you're able to reach. Sargent says, "If a CEO doesn't have the belief of his or her co-workers and the rest of the leadership team, there's no way they'll be effective."

Unless people are presented powerful and undeniable evidence to believe that you're different (better) than your predecessors, they'll either wink and whisper, "Here we go again," or adopt a deadly wait-and-see attitude.

Ask for It

The workplace has become a very cynical world, and that's totally understandable. During the past few decades employer loyalty to their work force has been replaced by the need to hit the current quarter's numbers at any cost. Workers believe they've been the victims of their leadership's infatuations with the latest management fads. They have watched their pensions disappear, have repeatedly been asked to sacrifice, and have then been repaid by being lied to or laid off. To assume that someone believes you because you've been named the boss is either naïve or arrogant.

When Fred Eppinger promised people he wasn't going to sell the company, shared his hopes for what could be accomplished, and asked people to set aside their cynicism, he made himself vulnerable. He was asking for their belief. In agreeing to do so, the workers also made themselves vulnerable and in that simple mutual act solid relationships began forming.

The only certain way to gain your employees' belief is to ask them for it.

Surround Yourself with Others Who *Will* Be Believed

An essential part of gaining and maintaining belief is getting rid of those managers who aren't believed or can't be believed. Yet many new leaders don't put "personal credibility" at the top of their list when deciding who should stay and who should go. Fred Eppinger is different.

"Shortly after I got here I went downstairs to see the head of marketing," says Eppinger, "and when I walked into her office I was dumbstruck by the fact that even though she'd been here more than two years, her office was absolutely empty. There wasn't a picture on the wall, no personal effects, only a desk and a chair. Clearly anybody who worked for her would be wondering why she didn't care enough about her job and the people she worked with to even hang a picture. It was just too weird." She had to go.

"The first time I met the man who was the president of our property and casualty divisions," Eppinger says, "we were in his office and I was struck by the fact that there was no whiteboard, no computer, nothing that would convince anyone that he was in business. When I started asking him about some of the numbers, he told me that he wasn't good on detail and that he wasn't familiar with the numbers I was asking about." Eppinger suggested that he spend some time familiarizing himself with them and that they'd meet again the following day.

"The next morning," says Eppinger, "I bumped into him in the elevator and he didn't have a briefcase with him so I assumed he had gotten in earlier than me. I said good morning and added, 'No briefcase, huh, you must have gotten in early,' to which he replied, 'No, I'm just getting in. I don't have a briefcase.'"

That divisional president didn't last long. If Eppinger was going to be believed, he couldn't afford to have a poseur who admitted to not knowing the numbers of his own unit.

Eppinger began the process of building a team of industry-leading talent who brought immediate credibility to the company. The team itself quickly became a valuable asset that helped attract even more talent to the company. Within a short amount of time, the undeniable buzz around the industry was that something special was going on at The Hanover.

Eppinger made open and honest communications a priority, reinforcing the company's proud history. This included intimate "breakfast with the CEO" meetings, video presentations, meetings with all new employees, and intranet news stories. And in every meeting and every communication, the messages were strong and consistent: "The Hanover is a company with a proud past and bright future, where all of its 4,000 employees are focused on a single goal, to be a world class property and casualty company, one that delivers value for all of its stakeholders—a company that is built to compete and win over the long term."

These key messages were consolidated into a booklet—"The Hanover Journey—Building a World Class Company Together"—which was designed to have employees across the company working off the same page, both literally and figuratively. It summarized the proud history of the company and described its current strong financial position. It presented a singular vision for the company, one that combines and balances its strategic priorities, core skills, and core values. And it laid out the company's distinctive value proposition for winning in the marketplace over the long term. And on the last page, Eppinger asked all employees to demonstrate their belief—to sign their names and sign on to the journey declaring their personal accountability for the company's continued growth and progress.

"Corporate presidents and chief executive officers, even the so-called smartest guys in the room, only are leaders to the degree that people choose to follow them," Eppinger says. "My personal contribution has been to help people connect with a clear vision of where we could go as a company and how we can get there, so that they want to be part of building something very special—something that will last a long time."

The Turnaround

Fred Eppinger managed to catch one lucky break during the time it took to make over the company. "Remember that $2 billion scythe hanging over our heads and that if every annuity holder had died on the same day we would have been bankrupt?" Fortunately for Eppinger the stock market began to strengthen, and he was able to hedge his going-forward liability and eventually gained the interest of two companies in acquiring the investments the annuity business had made.

"There were basically only two companies who could handle an acquisition of that size and I had to play one against the other," he says, "Lehman Brothers and Goldman Sachs. Neither of them wanted the business itself but they were interested in the investment portfolios. The way it worked was like this. The investments were worth $12 billion and the total potential liability (if and when every annuity holder died) was about $14 billion. Whoever bought it from us would be betting that the investments would increase in value and eventually be worth far more than the liabilities and the difference representing pure profit."

Lehman Brothers acquired the annuity business and by getting the $2 billion liability off his balance sheet, Eppinger was able to convince A. M. Best to raise his rating, which slowed the drain of business on the property and casualty side. Next, he got out of the broker dealer business and began concentrating on building a world-class property and casualty insurance company. The Hanover Group now ranks among the top thirty-five insurance companies in the nation. Under Eppinger's tutelage the company's share price has increased more than eleven times and the company possesses one of the cleanest balance sheets in the industry.

"I'm a pretty emotional guy," says Eppinger. "This was all about saving the company and making it great again for the community and the workers and we've done that. More than one thousand people have joined us from some of the finest companies in the industry and today our four thousand workers comprise one of the finest teams in the industry."

Perhaps the success Fred Eppinger came to enjoy as head of The Hanover Group was preordained. On paper he was the perfect candidate for the job. He'd grown up in the area and had a hardscrabble youth, parents who taught him how to persevere, and a fierce, deeply held pride in the community and the company. Professionally, he'd distinguished himself as one of the leading turnaround consultants in the insurance industry and further proven his value as a hands-on head at the Hartford Insurance Company straightening out their several billion dollar asbestos debacle.

But I'm not a believer in predestination. Plenty of others, all perfect candidates, take charge of troubled companies every year. Yet they flail and fail.

One thing is certain. Because Eppinger sensed the need and took the time and trouble to gain the belief of the people who would help him in rebuilding a broken but once great company, his chances for success were greatly improved. Today the foundation built by Fred Eppinger has proven to be rock solid. "I've got the best team in the world," he says. "We could run a company five times bigger, and one day we will. This is a $3 billion start-up!"

Hit the Ground Running Rule 2
Gain Belief

New leaders need the belief of the people they're asking to run alongside them. Leaders gain belief by:

- Being authentic and humble
- Getting rid of regal trappings
- Proving their worthiness
- Asking others for their belief
- Surrounding themselves with others who are also trusted

Rule 3: Ask for Help

"I'm the result of a lot of people who took the time during my career to kick me in the back side when I deserved it," says Howard Lance, CEO of Harris Corporation, early on during our first meeting at the company's Florida headquarters. I wondered if I'd finally ended up with one of the clichéd hardnosed CEOs I'd been expecting to meet during the research journey but I hadn't, and as it turned out . . . didn't.

"But more importantly," he says in a compassionate tone, "then they put an arm around my shoulder and helped me out, gave me their advice and support, and I'll never forget that as long as I live. They were the true mentors who taught me the value of asking for and being grateful for the help of others."

Lance says that when he arrived as the first outside CEO in the company's history, he found a solid foundation. "Harris was a good company with a rich history when I got here," he says, "but there was complacency and my challenge was to convince them they could become a great company."

It's not surprising that the company Lance took over had a bit of complacency. Although Harris had reinvented itself many times, it was already more than one hundred years old when he arrived, it had always been good (but not great) at what it did, the company offered reliable jobs that people were reluctant to leave, and "stable" would be the best word to describe the company.

Harris Corporation

Fewer than sixty miles away from where J. M. Smucker was tinkering with a way to speed up the process for making butter in Orrville, brothers Alfred and Charles Harris in Niles, Ohio, were doing some tinkering of their own. By 1890, the brothers, who owned a jewelry store but whose real passion was inventing things, had already lost a considerable amount of money on inventions including a twenty-four-hour clock and a nail-feeding machine, and they promised one another to stop inventing. But the inveterate inventors couldn't help themselves, and by 1895 they were convinced they had a winner.

Until that time printing presses had to be hand-fed one piece of paper at a time, but the brothers invented a machine that fed a printing press mechanically and could increase productivity ten times. So certain were the brothers that they finally had a viable product that they founded the Harris Automatic Press Company to market their invention.

Unfortunately, after listening to the brothers' sales pitch, nobody was willing to buy their machine. The brothers were bewildered. They couldn't understand how any printing company wouldn't want to increase their productivity ten times. Their dilemma was answered unexpectedly when a small printing company agreed to buy one of their machines if it could *double* their productivity. The brothers sold the company a machine and quickly revised their sales presentation.

Instead of promising prospective customers a tenfold increase in output, the brothers started promising that their productivity would double. Their business took off like a rocket. Before long happy customers were telling the brothers that their new machine was actually ten times faster than the old way. The brothers were hearing the exact same words they'd used in their sales pitch but which nobody had believed.

It's a lesson learned and still practiced more than one hundred years later at Harris; underpromise and overdeliver, whether talking about advanced communications solutions or financial forecasts. Underpromising and overdelivering is a great guiding principle applicable to everything in business, including when you're asking others to help you. Who would you be more willing to lend a helping hand—someone with a reputation for underpromising and overdelivering or someone with a reputation for doing the opposite?

Rapid innovation and key acquisitions during the next half century made the company one of the world's largest manufacturers of printing equipment. By the 1950s, the company had expanded its vision and decided to become a worldwide leader in all types of communications equipment. Through a rapid series of purchases the company became a leader in broadcast electronics and microwave radios. In 1967 it acquired Radiation Inc., a small Melbourne, Florida, company that specialized in space and military electronics, and the company quickly found itself playing a major role in America's space program.

In 1978 the company closed its Ohio headquarters and moved operations to Melbourne, Florida, which had become the technical heart of the company. After nearly one hundred years of being a major player in the printing business, the company sold off those interests in the 1980s and purchased General Electric's semiconductor division, which doubled its market share in the category. When the company celebrated its one hundredth birthday in 1995, it had become a diversified worldwide communications company in four categories: office systems, communications, semiconductors, and electronic systems.

By 2000 the company reinvented itself again by selling off the semiconductor and office systems divisions and focusing its resources on the global government and commercial communications equipment divisions. In 2003 the CEO who'd served the company for twenty-one years retired, and Howard Lance, former president and COO at NCR Corporation, took the reins as the firm's first outside CEO.

Howard Lance

Howard Lance's parents grew up in very large families living in modest houses and he doesn't think either of them completed high school. His father joined the Marines in World War II and served as a combat engineer until a shortage of pilots forced the military to create a unit called the Flying Sergeants. His father was commissioned as an officer, learned to fly, remained in the reserves following the war, and got called up for the Korean War, where he was shot down and received a medical discharge.

"My father worked very hard to provide a good home for our family. I don't think we were poor," says Lance, "probably more like lower middle class for the time and the town, East Peoria, Illinois, where we lived." His father ran heavy construction equipment and worked very hard to provide a good home for the family. He could be, says Lance, "one of the toughest and meanest former Marines you could ever know. We weren't close until I didn't have to live under his roof anymore and after that we were actually pretty good friends until he died when I was in my twenties.

"Still, it seemed that regardless of how well I did in school or sports it wasn't really good enough. I suppose," says Lance, "you could sum it up by saying I grew up with very traditional midwestern values," adding, "I developed a strong work ethic, an understanding that nobody is ever going to hand you anything and that you have to earn whatever you're going to get in life."

Lance says that all his relatives in East Peoria spent their careers in the building trades as steamfitters, bricklayers, and operating engineers. "While it wasn't that I didn't want to be like them, I instinctively knew I was always driven to do something different with my life."

Lance has a vivid recollection of one conversation with his father. "Three of my best friends were planning to attend college and I knew from a very early age that I wanted to go. The other parents had charted a course for their children's college educations but my family didn't see the value. When I sat down to discuss it with my father, his only response was that he couldn't afford to help me and suggested that I go to the local community college if I wanted to go to school."

Lance was fiercely determined to go to a four-year college and enrolled in a co-op engineering program at Bradley University that allowed him to work one semester at Caterpillar and then attend school the next semester. Upon graduation Lance was offered two jobs by Caterpillar: one in manufacturing operations and another one in product marketing. Because of his industrial engineering degree, Lance was urged to take the planning operations job but instead accepted the job in marketing.

"I'd spent my last summer assignment in the sales engineering department dealing with Caterpillar's customers and really loved it," he says. He ended up spending five years with the company in marketing and later in field assignments for the company in positions of increasing responsibility. "I was pretty naïve," he says, "in fact, when the company wanted to send me to San Diego in 1978 I actually had to get out a map to figure out where it was." Later there were other assignments in Los Angeles and Cleveland. Lance says he learned powerful lessons about customers and markets at Caterpillar.

"For whatever reason," Lance says, "I've always been the youngest at whatever I've done, so you can imagine what it was like being twenty-two years old and representing the company in front of their dealer organization composed of people old enough to be my father or grandfather. I was supposed to have all the answers for them and, as you might guess, the dealers had more than a little bit of fun with me.

"The big lesson that came out of that," he says, "was that I had to learn how to adapt to the situation," adding, "while some will argue that adaptability is a soft skill, I'd disagree and call it vital to success in business and life."

Lance says the most memorable lesson he learned at Caterpillar occurred when he went in to meet his supervisor for the first time. "Management trainees aren't really hired by the people they'll be working for," says Lance. "Instead, it's more like you're delivered to them. My first boss's name was Tom Vollertsen and when I walked into his office to meet him I was struck by a large plaque on his credenza which read, 'Activities are not the same as Results.'

"I've never forgotten that plaque, the message it implied, and I think of it often," he says, adding, "it's had a profound impact on my thinking and the setting of priorities to this day. It taught me that if you're keeping score, it isn't the hours you work or the effort you put into but instead it's about being successful at what you set out to achieve."

When Lance left Caterpillar he joined a division of Emerson Electric Company, a global manufacturing company with 265 manufacturing sites worldwide, and spent the next 17 years there and learned the lessons, he says, that prepared him to be a successful CEO. "Everything I know about management, process, and strategy," he says, "I learned at Emerson, where I had tremendous mentors who helped and guided me."

During his time at Emerson Lance progressed from being an individual contributor to a manager, supervisor, general manager, president, and finally group executive. He says, "I'd still be there if there had been a chance to become CEO." Unfortunately for Lance there was someone else at the company two years his senior who'd preceded him in most of the jobs he held. "When David Farr got the job as CEO in 2000," Lance says, "I knew that if I wanted to be a CEO I'd have to leave the company."

He also cites an overseas assignment as his baptism by fire that prepared him to lead a global company like Harris by exposing him to different cultures and challenges. "One day," he says, "Chuck Knight, the CEO and chairman of the company, called me into his office and told me the company had a big problem in Hong Kong and asked me to go live there and fix it. He told me I'd be the only other person in the company with a CEO title and running a publicly owned entity and that it would be a great opportunity for me."

A mess awaited Lance in Hong Kong. The company he was asked to take over had manufacturing operations all over the world and was publicly traded in London, and the controlling shareholder (Emerson) was in St. Louis. The Asian financial markets tumbled as soon as he took over, the company's share price fell precipitously and demand for the company's products tanked. Lance says he spent all his time circling the globe trying to placate outside directors, majority owners, and stock market analysts and working to keep the leadership team in place and grow the company.

There was a lot of animosity among the non-Emerson management in the company, everyone's stock options were underwater, and it became apparent that the best resolution was for Emerson to buy the publicly traded portion of the company, which it eventually did. "I won't take full credit for it," says Lance, "but I kept everyone in the game until we got it resolved, I didn't lose a single executive during the process, and that company has gone on to be a great success for Emerson. Without that experience," he says, "I'm not sure the Harris board of directors would have considered me for their CEO."

Lance credits his Asian experience with changing his life in many ways. "Your perspective on everything changes," he says. "I tell every young person I meet that they should hope I'll ask them to accept an international assignment and promise them it will be more positive than negative and will change them forever."

Upon the successful completion of his Asian mission, Emerson asked Lance to move back to St. Louis and head another group. "By that time I figured out the other guy was going to get the CEO slot and I'd just be going back and doing more of the same all over again." He says, "I'd still be there if there had been a chance to become CEO." Instead, Lance accepted an offer from Lars Nyberg to take the role of president and COO of the retail and financial group at NCR. Lance says Nyberg and the board of directors made it very clear they were looking for a CEO successor.

Howard Lance believes that his experience at NCR was the biggest failure of his career and also his most instructive. The culture he found at NCR was highly charged politically and different than anything he'd previously encountered. "It was not a very pleasant experience," he says. "The people were capable and motivated but the company was broken far beyond what I expected.

"At Emerson what you saw was what you got," he says, "and everyone knew and played by the same rules but I never quite figured out the different rules for different people at NCR. I knew how to fix the business, but never figured out the politics. I was a *fish out of water* and finally figured out that it wasn't going to work. I went home and told my wife I was leaving."

Lance muses that something good frequently comes on the heels of something bad and believes the door was opened for him to become CEO of a major company because of his decision to leave NCR. Named CEO of Harris in January 2003 it was time for the most important transition in Howard Lance's career.

Ask for Help

When Howard Lance became CEO of Harris he faced some big hurdles that could have kept him from succeeding.

- He was the first outside CEO in the company's 107-year history.

- A very capable and popular internal candidate didn't get the job.

- The company was in good shape and his turnaround skills weren't required.

- Almost half of the company's 16,000 workers are scientists and engineers, folks widely acknowledged as being difficult to manage and skeptical about almost everything that can't be proven on a chalkboard.

- Much evidence shows that the performance of outside CEOs lags far behind CEOs promoted from within.

But he also knew there was tremendous upside potential. "This was a good company," he says, "but I think most of the people here would agree that it was no longer a great company. Maybe it had been at one point, but it wasn't any longer. There was a lack of growth, complacency, and a lot of inward perspective on how good we were. I was excited about the possibility of playing a role that would make Harris great again.

"The immediate opportunity existed to put strong processes in place for strategic planning," says Lance, "plus there were huge opportunities to drive new growth in both the government and commercial businesses. Another big opportunity existed in driving international growth, but most important this was a chance to come in, create a spark, and possibly be a catalyst for people to step back and say, 'Wow, we can really do this!'"

As Lance weighed the positives and the negatives he realized that to hit the ground running he'd need to get lots of help. Lance systematically set out to ask the board, the executive team, and his fellow co-workers for their help.

Ask Your Bosses for Help

Howard Lance knew he had to get everyone on his side, and he started with the board of directors. "The first thing I did was ask all seven members of our board who were or had been CEOs to become my mentors," Lance says. "I went to each of them and said, 'I know a lot of aspects about being a CEO but you've been a successful one and I don't want to make mistakes that you've already learned about along life's way.' "

"I explained to each of them that I wanted to view the board of directors as a resource, not a threat. After all, the worst thing a board can ever do is fire you."

His request for help was a brilliant move on Lance's part: It demonstrated a degree of vulnerability. Nora Klaver, the author of *May Day! Asking for Help in Times of Need,* says, "There are many reasons people fear requesting assistance, primary among them not wanting to seem weak, needy, or incompetent."

In large measure the fear of asking for help is the fault of everyone who sits on boards, analyzes markets, and invests in companies. "Wall Street likes a man on a white horse," Michael Metz, the longtime chief investment strategist for Oppenheimer & Co., told me. "This is the era of the great heroic figure and Wall Street encourages investors to look for someone with great talent who by himself can turnaround a multi-billion dollar company."

Of course that man on a white horse exists only in fairy tales. Yet the average top executive finds the image irresistible and routinely goes to great lengths to keep up appearances. Topping the list is to always look large and in charge, never in doubt, with no need for help, and confidently in control.

Keeping up the appearance of power can turn tragic. In the post-mortem following CEO Stan O'Neal's firing at Merrill Lynch, one knowledgeable insider told Randall Smith of the *Wall Street Journal* that more than anything the directors were surprised by the size of the loss. He should have communicated, the insider explained, but O'Neal didn't walk the board through the reasons.

Garret Keizer, author of *Help: The Original Human Dilemma,* goes one step further and writes, "There's a tendency in business to act as if a request for help is a deficiency . . . there's an understandable fear that if you let your guard down, you'll be hurt, or that the information you don't know will be used against you. That's so short-sighted. Most individuals want and need to help others and derive pleasure from doing so."

There are many lessons to be learned from getting the board of directors on your side, even if your "board of directors" isn't a formal one. Everybody either reports to someone or has a group of people to whom they're responsible.

If you're a solo entrepreneur, family members, the people who provided help with financing, or a trusted group of advisers should be viewed as your board. If you're a department manager in a company, your bosses or the people you report to should be seen as yours.

Ask Co-workers for Help

"People inside a company see a lot more than they're sometimes given credit for," Lance says. "People instinctively know whether another person is genuine and that's a problem with a lot of imperial, larger than life CEOs. They often appear powerful with all their personal charisma but frequently that's superficial."

By contrast, during his first one hundred days at Harris, Howard Lance did a lot of listening and very little answering. He knew that getting everyone on his side would determine the future success of his tenure and the company. He needed to develop credibility with the new team.

"I needed to be accepted here," says Lance. "People had to know I was committed, that I truly believed it was about all of us together winning as a team and I also wanted them to get to know me as person." He says, "I began by working my tail off and started earlier and finished later than everyone else. People needed to personally witness the level of my commitment."

Workers couldn't envision themselves on a winning team with Lance if they were fearful for their jobs, so one of his first orders of business was to let people know their jobs were safe. "Everyone assumed I'd come in and clean house," he says. "After all, the conventional wisdom is that new CEOs need to remake their leadership teams . . . fast. But I had no intention of doing that. There were a lot of very talented people here."

Lance says that the CFO, head of HR, and the general counsel were all in their early sixties and each assumed they'd be cut loose immediately. "I had no intention of putting anyone out to pasture," he says. "Each of them was very talented and they had the tribal knowledge and the history of the company."

Tribal knowledge is an often underappreciated and undervalued asset, especially by outsiders. It's not the stuff of process manuals or HR training. Tribal knowledge is the gut understanding of how things get done and what can hold you back. It understands the workarounds, the maneuvers, and the location of the hidden obstacles to implementing anything big or small. It includes the history of the company, the complex relationships between people, and the issues than can derail good ideas. Tribal knowledge is as unique as DNA and just as important.

As one example, Lance cites the case of Bob Henry. "When I became CEO Bob was in charge of government communications systems, our biggest division. He was an expert in government markets and I wasn't. He'd also been the internal candidate for the CEO position and everyone was guessing he'd leave the company or that I'd get rid of him. Instead," says Lance, "I made it goal number one to try and forge a great personal relationship with him," adding, "he has incredible talents I don't have and maybe I possess a few he doesn't have but we've become great friends, terrific colleagues, and we've learned a lot from each other."

Lance got to know people by listening and engaging people at all levels of the organization and those people got to know him. He believes that "listening brings involvement, which brings understanding, which ultimately brings commitment."

Considering how many managers tell me that their company fails to get the full involvement and commitment of people, it's clear that many leaders aren't that good at listening. It's understandable. Listening takes a huge investment of time and energy—the two most precious assets of any top leader. First, the leader needs to ask good questions and that takes preparation. And second, people hear and comprehend four times faster than even the most articulate people can talk. So it takes incredible discipline and concentration to keep one's mind from racing ahead and missing critical input.

The private meetings Lance held with hundreds of people during the first three months weren't only an exchange of pleasantries and idle chitchat. "During our conversations," Lance says, "I asked a lot of questions." Some of the questions Lance asked included:

- How do you think we're doing as a company?

- How do you think your area of the company is doing?

- What do you think about our revenue growth? Is it sufficient?

- How do you think our profit margins are doing?

- What should we do to grow your division?

- What should we do to grow profits?

- What are the things that hold us back as an organization?

- Do you think we can do better?

Lance says that "everyone agreed the company could be doing much better and almost everyone said, 'We've been waiting for someone to come along and show us the way.'"

Lance's instincts were right on target. What makes engineers, scientists, and other professionals difficult to manage is also what makes them professionals. They are highly educated, driven, and a lot more critical than the average employee. Some managers find these people intimidating and often fake equal expertise or exercise their authority as "the boss." Those two tactics always backfire. Instead of getting defensive or asserting his dominance, Lance asked questions (professionals love to show their expertise) and showed respect by admitting he needed their help (professionals are problem solvers and will jump at a chance to help).

"I would never disparage any of my predecessors," he says, "because each was probably the right person for the right time in the company's history. But I frequently consider how fortunate I was to be chosen to be here at my right time for the next chapter in the Harris story. Everybody was ready to grow and win."

As Lance's first hundred days were drawing to a close it was time for the company's annual management conference, where leaders got together to discuss the past and coming year and its prospects. Before Lance's arrival the meeting was generally attended by the top ten or fifteen people in the company.

"It takes more than ten or fifteen people to run a global company," says Lance. "I wanted people from all across all the business units to be there. Many of these executives had never even met one another before. For my presentation I used a series of financial charts to show everyone what I thought we could do and become and explained to them that I believed it was possible. Then I told them that if they'd join me in believing it was possible—that together—we could make it happen."

Lance has a keen sense of humor and doesn't have a problem generating a laugh even at his own expense. "Sometimes you have to take off the veneer and let people see you for who you really are and share a chuckle or two.

"It turned out to be a great meeting," he says, "and as the conference was coming to a close I had them turn up the music and put on a hit song from the 1980s by Timbuk 3, a group nobody's heard from since."

Suddenly the company's new CEO was on stage wearing a pair of sunglasses, dancing, and lip syncing the words to "The Futures So Bright, I Gotta Wear Shades." "People looked at one another," he says, "as if to ask, 'What's going on with this guy,' and then laughter erupted, the clapping started, and everyone had a blast."

Predictably, by the end of the conference, e-mail and text messages were flying throughout the company reporting on the new CEO's performance and most carried messages like this from one executive to another:

Marie, the new CEO just finished dancing on stage and singing that the future's so bright he has to wear sunglasses. The guy's one of us. Things are going to be OK. We're all in the same boat! Dan

Howard Lance had successfully achieved the mission. He had the board and the management team on his side. "Then it was time," he says, "to roll up our sleeves, hit the ground running, and build a great company."

How Other CEOs Asked for Help

Mike McCallister, CEO of Humana, was working as a finance person at a small hospital when he got his first job as the acting administrator of a tiny hospital. "There was a woman who worked in the administrator's office who took one look at me and sensed I didn't know what I was doing," he says, "and one day, she finally said to me, 'Don't worry, hon, I'll show you how to do it,' and every day after that she spent a couple hours a day teaching me how to run a hospital." McCallister, who has stayed in contact with his helpmate, says she became the hospital's CFO soon after he left and is still on the job.

One of Pat Hassey's first decisions when he took over as CEO at troubled Allegheny Technologies was to call the company's top four executives into his office and tell them their jobs were safe but that he needed their help. "I told them," he says, "that a big part of their job was to tell me what to do and provide me advice and guidance. I promised them that every opinion would count and that no decisions would be made until I'd heard all their opinions."

Marshall Larsen, CEO of Goodrich, says that any accomplished business leader has to count on other people and be up front about asking for help. "What I need to have are people who aren't afraid to look me in the eye and tell me I'm wrong," he says. "Unless a CEO asks for the help of others," he adds, "and is prepared to listen to the people around him, eventually the organization will suffer from 'group think' and he'll lead them all off a cliff like lemmings."

Ron Sargent, CEO of Staples, says, "We have a very active board. At various times we've had Meg Whitman, former CEO of eBay; Senator Mitchell from Maine; Mitt Romney; and Brenda Barnes, the former head of Sara Lee." While no board will ever be as knowledgeable about the day-to-day operations of a company as the management, their help as a sounding board is indispensable. "To make certain I get as much help from them as possible," Sargent says, "I begin every board meeting by saying, 'Here are the things that are on my mind and I'd love some input from you on what you think.'"

No One Can Go It Alone

Michael Metz, who has observed CEOs and their track records for more than three decades, explained that this idea of "some white knight" turning a company around singlehandedly is relatively new. "When I got started," Metz says, "there wasn't the feeling that one man genius would turn things around. It was a feeling you had to have a complete management structure in place and that would determine whether the company was successful or not."

Business guru Warren Bennis says this misconception is due to the "peoplefication" of our thinking. "The lone hero gallops through our imagination . . . shouting commands, decreeing the compelling vision, and leading the way with brio and shimmer." But the most urgent projects, those that will build a different business for a different future (like Lance did), require the input and contributions of many talented people. Bennis concludes that the most successful new leaders are "great connoisseurs of talent."

"Remember how I told you that one of my biggest business lessons was about the need to get results?" Lance asked me. "Well, let me add a corollary to that lesson—you'll get the results you want more effectively if you get people on your team."

As we discussed the need for getting people on your side, Lance leaned back, smiled, and said, "I promise that if you ask anyone who knew me twenty years ago if I was someone who'd ask for help they'd laugh and say, 'That's not the Howard we remember,' and they'd tell you I was always the hard charger shouting 'Out of my way' and too busy climbing the ladder to ask for help.

"I'm a different person today than I was twenty years ago," says Lance, "and one of the big reasons is because I learned to ask for help along the way. Otherwise I wouldn't be sitting in this chair today." His strategy is working. During Lance's first five years as CEO of Harris, the company's revenues have nearly tripled, profits have increased fivefold, and the stock price has increased by 260 percent.

Hit the Ground Running Rule 3
Ask for Help

Effective leaders recognize that they need the help of everyone around them in order to make their leadership a success. They're secure enough to ask for it and humble enough to make use of it. Here are Howard Lance's rules for asking for help:

- Admit you don't have all the answers.
- Put aside your ego and gain the knowledge of others.
- Listen to people, learn the tribal knowledge, and get influential employees on your side.
- Turn your bosses (including boards of directors) into advisers and strategic resources.

Rule 4: Find, Keep, and Grow the Right People

If you're ever in one of Staples several thousand stores and a trim, enthusiastic, and bespectacled associate introduces himself and helps you out, check his name tag. If it says "Ron" and he has a moustache, it's probably Ron Sargent, CEO of the $28 billion giant.

If you think working in stores several days a week meeting with associates and greeting customers is beneath the CEO of the world's largest office supply superstore, think again. "You need to remember," laughs Sargent, "that for a guy who started out in Boston scrubbing toilets forty hours a week, working in stores helping our workers and customers was a big promotion."

When asked to list the giant retailer's most important assets, Sargent responds, without pause, "Only two things really count at Staples: our customers and our people who deliver the customer service experience." While Sargent was serving as the number two executive at Staples he'd patiently created a list of what he would do if and when he got the top job. As you'll learn, his list ensured he'd be ready if and when the opportunity arrived for him to become the firm's CEO.

Staples

In 1985, while most of Boston was celebrating a hot and sticky Fourth of July weekend, Tom Stemberg, an out-of-work supermarket executive, was sweating over a business proposal when his printer ribbon broke. Because the holiday that year fell at the end of the week, all the local stationary and office supply stores were closed for a long weekend. As he drove aimlessly around the suburbs trying to find an open store, Stemberg had a sudden epiphany. What the world needed, he realized, was a big honking office supply store that looked and felt a lot like a supermarket with convenient operating hours.

Many entrepreneurs are encouraged to follow their passion. Stemberg says, "I think following your passion is a stupid idea. I know a lot of people who followed their passion and ended up with bankrupt restaurants and golf courses. Instead of following your passion, find a great market that provides an opportunity to truly satisfy customers and make money."

Stemberg found his money partner in Leo Kahn, a veteran of the grocery business, and within ten months they had opened the first Staples store in Brighton, Massachusetts. The wild race was on with few pauses for breath during the next twenty years.

If Stemberg's idea for an office supply superstore had occurred in an earlier time, he might have been able to open a few stores, perfect distribution, work out the bugs, build a history of consistent profitability, model desired customer service standards, and then begin an orderly expansion. He didn't have that luxury.

As word spread that a hot new retail concept had taken off in Massachusetts and that a typical store was doing $60,000 a week in revenues, copycat competitors started sprouting up like weeds. Within only two years Staples had more than twenty direct competitors scattered across the United States with names like HQ Office,

Office Stop, Office America, Office World, Business Depot, Office Depot, and OfficeMax. Each vowed to be the biggest, best, and last one standing, so Staples had to scale quickly or risk becoming a New England anomaly.

Within two years of opening its first store and with the help of Mitt Romney, then a partner of Bain & Company, Staples went public and began madly spending the money they'd raised on store expansion, acquisition, and hiring. The company quickly opened stores in the Midwest that floundered at first, but the company still moved on to California snapping up rivals along the way. In 1989 it launched its catalog delivery service, which the company expects to become its biggest source of revenue in the next several years. Within only five years of its founding, Staples opened its first Canadian store and partnered with British retail giant Kingfisher to open stores in the United Kingdom.

By the company's tenth anniversary, it was opening its five hundredth store, had already become a *Fortune* 500 company, and e-commerce was beginning to take off at Staples.com. Ron Sargent, the company's current chairman and CEO, says it was a land grab. "It was a race. At one point we were opening a new store every forty-two hours in order to stake out the territory before a competitor got there." Only five years later, as Staples prepared to celebrate its fifteenth birthday, the company was opening its one thousandth store and sales topped $10 billion for the first time.

"It was all about growth," says Sargent, "and while growth has served us well I'm not sure it was always profitable growth." He says, "We stumbled badly and lost money in Europe for more than a decade just for the sake of saying we were there and for a long time we didn't make any money with Staples.com but kept our foot firmly on the accelerator."

As the nation entered a recession in the year 2000, the company's growth began slowing, the dot-com bubble burst, and the company began acknowledging that perhaps it had grown too quickly and that it was time to reassess. At the same time, the focus of Tom Stemberg, the company's founder, who'd excelled at being a growth-oriented entrepreneur, began to drift.

Stemberg, who'd made hundreds of millions of dollars from his stock in Staples, began showing an increasing lack of interest in the day-to-day management of a huge company and became preoccupied with his new interests including a start-up flower store franchise concept and a dry cleaning idea called Zoots.

In September of 2001, Stemberg passed the CEO reins to his number two, Ron Sargent, COO and president, who'd been with the company almost since its inception.

Ron Sargent

Ron Sargent vividly remembers the day in August 1973 when he boarded his first airplane and flew from his small hometown in Kentucky to Boston, Massachusetts. He was eighteen and had been accepted at Harvard.

"I landed in Boston with all my belongings and a thick ole' boy Kentucky accent and had to figure out how to get from the airport to the campus. When I'd stop people and ask them how to get to Harvard," he recalls, "they weren't very helpful. They'd take one look at me, decide I was a hillbilly, and start mumbling stuff about having to take a subway. Nobody bothered to tell me that I had to take a bus to get to the subway.

"After a lot of buses and subways and moving back and forth on inbounds, out bounds, red lines, green lines, and blue lines, I finally found Harvard Square," he says, "and as I made my way to the top of the stairs I was greeted by a big group of Hare Krishna's chanting and playing their finger cymbals. I'd never been on an airplane, never been in a subway, and had certainly never seen a Hare Krishna. I felt as though I'd ended up in a different universe.

"Most of my family were tobacco farmers in central Kentucky," says Sargent, "but after World War II my father decided he didn't want to spend his life on a farm and headed for the *big* city of Covington, where be became a mechanic." Sargent's mother was a housewife and both parents were focused on their two children receiving good educations.

"The high school I went to wasn't very good," he says, "and it was fairly easy for me to do well," adding that even today fewer than 15 percent of the students who attend Holmes High School go on to college. "I was accepted at the University of Kentucky," he says, "but took a chance and also applied to Harvard and was accepted."

At the time it cost $5,000 a year to attend Harvard, and Sargent wasn't sure he'd be able to swing it. "At the time my father was making $11,000 a year before taxes but agreed to kick in $1,000," he says. "I borrowed $1,500, earned another $1,000 on a summer job, and Harvard gave me a $750 scholarship. I was able to scrape together enough money for one year and figured I'd go for it and see what would happen."

"Besides the small scholarship," he says, "Harvard promised me a great job on something called the Dorm Crew." Sargent's job during his freshman year was cleaning toilets, but his assignments became progressively better after that. "By my sophomore year I was a janitor, the third year I was a garbage man, and in my senior year I delivered the mail."

Sargent says he regrets not having had more fun during his undergraduate years at Harvard. "It was tough for me," he admits. "A phone call back home was something I could only afford to do on Sundays." He spent Thanksgivings alone in an empty dorm room while his more affluent classmates were able to go home.

"Harvard was intimidating," he says. "There's a lot of wealth and privilege there and I was the guy who wasn't able to join people for the big Saturday nights out in Boston because I just didn't have any money. Maybe all Harvard freshmen are insecure," he says, "but I remember thinking that maybe I was the only admissions mistake Harvard had ever made."

Sargent knew he wanted a career in business, so he majored in economics and by his senior year decided to immediately go to work on an MBA. "Most people get their undergraduate degree and then work for a few years before going back to get an MBA, but I wasn't sure I'd ever make it back, so I decided to do it right away.

"I remember a conversation with my dad about my decision to apply to business school," says Sargent. "He'd never really understood my decision to go to Harvard when I could have had a free ride at the University of Kentucky and there I was telling him I was going to borrow another $20,000 and spend two more years in school. He thought he had a professional student for a son who would never get a job and earn his keep."

But Sargent was determined and applied to business schools at both Harvard and Stanford, making it clear on his applications that he was going to start his MBA studies the following year one way or another and that this was his single shot. Stanford told him to work for a few years first, but Harvard accepted him and he went to work on his graduate degree.

As a twenty-one year old studying for an MBA alongside seasoned and accomplished classmates who'd spent time in the workplace, Sargent found business school very challenging. "I didn't have the background and experience that my classmates had," he says, "but I had great study habits, took what I was doing more seriously than most of them, and within six months I knew I'd make it."

Every summer throughout college Sargent would head back to Kentucky where he'd live at home to save money and work in the home office of the Kroger Company, one of the nation's largest grocery store chains. When he graduated with his MBA, he received six job offers including one from Kroger and another from Neiman Marcus. "The offer from Neiman Marcus was intriguing," he says.

"They talked about buying trips around the world and all kinds of fun stuff while Kroger said I'd be spending the first eight months cutting up cows and chickens and trimming produce." He decided to accept the offer from Kroger where he'd spend the first ten years of his career.

"I took Kroger's offer," he says, "because all the other MBAs were going into consulting and investment banking and I thought there'd be great opportunities for someone with an MBA in retail and because there were only a handful of MBAs in the company, so I thought I'd advance quickly."

"I was treated well at Kroger," he says, adding that he recently joined the board of directors, "and got to do a lot of things while I was there but over time came to realize that the company had what I call *gray hair syndrome*. At the time you were supposed to be a store manager for ten years because everyone else had been a store manager for ten years. Next you were supposed to be a zone manager for five years because that's what everyone else before you had done. I made it to director of dairy marketing (one level below a vice president) in only ten years," he says, "but remember thinking that it would take another ten years to get to the next level."

Sargent credits Kroger with teaching him a lot of lessons that have served him well. "I learned how a big company works and I learned how to do things right, but it was just a little too slow for me and too hard to make an impact."

Sargent's break came in the form of a phone call from a former Kroger executive who'd become a headhunter. "He told me he represented a company that wanted to open stores in the Midwest and invited me to come to Boston for an interview. I wasn't interested in the least," he says, but admits, "the idea of an expense paid trip to Boston was intriguing and I'd get to catch up with old friends from my days at Harvard." The headhunter who called was representing Staples, which at the time had fifteen stores in the Northeast.

"I visited store number one and store number two," says Sargent, "toured their distribution center and remember thinking they were on to something really good. The more I thought about it the more interested I became. I was only thirty-three years old at the time. My career at Kroger was moving along at the speed of a glacier; I was engaged but still single and decided, 'If I'm ever going to take a flier, now is the time.'"

What Sargent liked most about the concept was what he calls the replenishable nature of the stores. "One of the great things about the grocery business," he says, "is that you might have good days and bad days but the reality is that people have to eat. I realized it was the same thing with office supplies. People are going to use up what they've purchased and have no choice but to replace them."

Sargent said yes and agreed to join Staples as a regional vice president responsible for opening stores in the Midwest. "My father, my fiancé, and the people I worked with at Kroger thought I was nuts," he says. "They couldn't imagine why I'd go to work for a company that wasn't public, wasn't making any money, and only had fifteen stores."

Sargent's first assignment at Staples was to open twenty stores in the Midwest within his first twelve months. "We got to five stores and kind of stalled," he explains. "While the average store in the Northeast was doing $60,000 a week, the Midwest stores were only averaging $30,000 in weekly sales. I got a call from the person who was the president at the time and he said, 'We thought the Midwest was going to be the next hot area but now we think it's going to be California,' and asked me to go there."

Sargent had gotten married and didn't want to head to California but agreed to fill a position in Boston. Within a year the company decided to begin a delivery business; Sargent raised his hand and it became his claim to fame.

"We started delivering out of the back of stores," he says, "and quickly created a catalog, call centers, distribution centers and within a couple of years decided we wanted to serve bigger customers and purchased seven large companies that specialized in that business and integrated them." Staples delivery business currently accounts for 40 percent of its total revenue, and Sargent estimates that by 2013 it will account for more revenue than the company's retail stores. In 1997, in acknowledgment of the work he'd done in successfully launching the delivery service, Sargent was promoted to president and COO, a position he held until it was announced that he would become the second CEO in the history of the company.

Other than the announcement, made a week before 9/11, that Sargent would become Staple's next CEO, nothing in 2001 went well for the company. Staples tried to create a separate class of tracking stock aside from its regular shareholders (something Sargent opposed but says it wasn't his call to make) and got sued. For the first time in the company's history same-store sales were down, the stock price tumbled from $18 to $11 a share, and the economy was in a recession.

"I remember thinking to myself," Sargent says, "'The good news is I finally get to be the CEO; the bad news is I'm walking in the footprints of a legend and things couldn't be in worse shape.' It wasn't a bad company," he's quick to add, "but there were lots of things that had to get cleaned up and fixed and I was the guy who had to do it.

"The results we achieved in 2001 were predictable," says Sargent. "Throughout the nineties we were moving as fast as humanly possible and mistakes got made along the way. In order to fill the stores with workers we'd hired almost anyone. Inside the company we called it *warm body syndrome*. We had a lot of executives who might have been right for a $100 million company but weren't right for a $10 billion enterprise and," he admits frankly, "we didn't have a good customer service culture. Toss in a recession and it's not surprising we had a bad year.

"During my years in the number two role," says Sargent, "I'd always kept a list of things I'd do if I got the top job," adding, "it was a long list. The challenge was figuring out which of the things I'd do during the first hundred days and which ones I'd handle in the longer term." Deciding which items on Sargent's list would get addressed first was made easier by virtue of one of his first acts as heir apparent: commissioning an outside research firm to provide Staples an honest assessment of where it stood in the minds of its customers.

The study revealed that consumers thought Staples's prices were okay but not great, found its store format dated, thought that its stores had become too "consumerish," that it had lost its office products appeal, and that nothing distinguished it from its competitors. As Fred Eppinger, of The Hanover Group, says, "Nobody ever wants to admit their baby is ugly but sometimes it's necessary."

How Sargent Hit the Ground Running

Sargent makes a persuasive case that a new person in charge has to move quickly and decisively in order to be effective. "I think a lot of people get intimidated by the role they've taken and say to themselves, 'I'm going to take some time and settle in, learn the job, and do my research over the first year,'" adding, "if you wait too long you'll lose everybody and your opportunity to effect change will be gone. I think a new leader has to do something big, new, and different within the first one hundred days and make sure that it's properly communicated to everyone. If people don't know what's going on," he warns, "they'll assume nothing is going on.

"Symbolic gestures were always very important to me and I think they are to most people," says Sargent. "A leader needs to quickly be able to say, 'Here's the five-point plan we're going to concentrate on during the next year.'"

Titled *Back to Brighton* (the site of the original store), the plan Sargent came up with and began communicating to the organization included:

- Shuttering unprofitable stores

- Cutting the number of items sold in the stores

- Creating a shopping experience for Staples's core business customer

- Implementing a new store format

- Creating the Staples's Foundation to support local communities

Store Closings

"I'm a straightforward and fairly simple guy," he says, "and we had to simplify, stop any bleeding, and get rid of stuff that didn't make sense or wasn't profitable for the company.

"I visited the thirty-one stores we closed," says Sargent. "It wasn't the fault of the employees that we were closing them and they deserved an explanation. Each store represented a mistake on the part of management. Either we'd made a bad real estate decision or we'd run the store poorly. It meant a lot of people lost jobs because of our errors in judgment and that didn't feel good."

Merchandise Reduction

The winning formula for a retailer is simple. You need to get the right merchandise, in the right place, for the right price, at the right time. But achieving "simple" is oh so difficult in business.

"Probably the toughest decision," Sargent remembers, "and one that didn't go down well with our merchants, was my decision to cut eight hundred items out of each store. Merchants like more items [because] more items mean more sales.

"Our core business customer is where we earn a profit," Sargent continues, "and that meant we had to lose the Brittany Spears backpacks, the fluorescent pens, and all the consumer stuff. We needed to get rid of the tchotchkes that were clogging up the stores." He adds, "We weren't telling consumers not to visit our stores but we couldn't pander to them at the risk of losing our business customers.

"By getting rid of those eight hundred items we were able to expand product lines that were very important to our small business customers and it meant we had greater depth of stock in the things they needed." In other words, they went from having more items to more of the right items.

The immediate result was that sales stayed flat and didn't go down as every merchant feared. The company's gross margin (profit before operating expenses) actually went up, which proved beneficial to the hammering it had been taking from Wall Street analysts.

A Sincere Commitment to Customer Service

"After becoming CEO I met with all our operators," says Sargent, "and one of them asked my three biggest priorities. My answer was 'customer service, customer service, customer service.' I explained that any of our competitors would be able to copy our store design, product mix, and pricing but that if we could differentiate ourselves in customer service it would propel us to be great."

Sargent says he immediately changed some people, too. "If we were going to be serious about our customer service initiative," he says, "we had to move operationally oriented people out of customer service." Another big decision by Sargent was to stop focusing on what the competition was doing, something that many business mangers and executives waste time on. "I told everyone that I didn't want any energy or effort spent on what the competition was doing or any time wasted constantly comparing our performance to others. I wanted all our time and talents dedicated to us, our stores, and the customer service experience we were delivering."

Many companies routinely announce new initiatives with lots of fanfare but fail to put any muscle into them and months later wonder what happened to them. The Staples's customer service plan put forth by Sargent had teeth.

Each Staples location was measured monthly by its revenues and profits but also by mystery shoppers who measured how the store was doing in its adherence to the new customer service program. Mystery shopper programs are administered by independent firms that hire people and pay them to visit a store (or a series of a stores in a chain), interact with the staff and present challenging questions to them, and buy merchandise. Based on their findings, the stores being evaluated receive a numerical ranking, and outstanding individual customer service is also noted. Companies use these results to improve their overall customer satisfaction ranking. Staples elected to offer bonus money to the staff of high-achieving stores.

"The money was shared by everyone in the store," says Sargent, "and even for a part-time sixteen-year-old worker it could easily mean an extra $50 a month, which was big money to them."

New Store Format

"When they're shopping for office products," Sargent says, "people don't want the hassle of shopping at Walmart, and they don't want to buy pens and paper at Costco stuck behind some guy with two flatbeds of food for his restaurant."

Staples's new store format was designed to provide the small business customer an easier and faster shopping experience. "Research showed that getting into the store, easily finding what they wanted, and getting out quickly," says Sargent, "was even more important to them than price. So we got rid of the warehouse style pallets and racks and created a racetrack design that allowed people to get around the stores easier, find what they were looking for, and check out fast."

The Staples Foundation

"By the time we hit $10 billion in annual sales," says Sargent, "I felt we had an obligation to give back to the communities and during my first month we created the Staples Foundation. There are two schools of thought regarding business and charitable giving. One is that the purpose of business is to make money for the shareholders and that it's not management's job to tell them what to do with *their* money. The other," he says, "is that we'd made a lot of people wealthy, we're a high-profile company, and we're honor bound to give back to our communities."

Prior to Sargent's initiative, corporate giving had been limited to providing groups and civic organizations a handful of gift certificates or dollar-off coupons when asked for support. "We decided we couldn't do everything for everyone and decided to begin by focusing on providing educational opportunities for disadvantaged youth and began with a million-dollar annual commitment through the Boys & Girls Clubs of America." The Staples Foundation has expanded and currently contributes more than $7 million annually to a number of causes that the company's work force is instrumental in selecting.

"While I knew it was important and the right thing to do," he says, "I hadn't fully gauged how important it was for our employees. It really served as a good reminder to me that people don't work just to earn a paycheck. People need to feel good about the companies they work for and feel like they're making a difference in the world." Sargent says, "It was extraordinarily uplifting inside the company and explosive in a positive way," revealing his pride at one of the imprimaturs he's made on the company. "Giving charitable organizations a handful of $10-off merchandise coupons to use in our stores just didn't cut it!"

Finding, Keeping, and Growing the Right People

Any successful business leader will tell you that the biggest challenge in business is finding, keeping, and growing the right people, and the key to doing it successfully is by making the right people feel like they're part of a special team. People don't quit teams; they only quit *organizations* and Ron Sargent has mastered the art of turning an organization into a team.

"The 94,000 people who make up our team are the heart of this company," says Sargent. "They're the reason we're able to provide exemplary customer service and ultimately earn a profit for our shareholders."

But, at the same time, he makes it abundantly clear that slackers need not apply. "You need to invite people on board one at a time," he says, "and enlist them in what you're trying to do and where you're trying to go. But the other part of that equation is making it clear that people are either on the train or they're not and if it's their choice not to take the train they have to get out of the station.

"People always talk about how difficult it is to fire someone," Sargent says, but, with a note of careful reflection in his voice, adds, "and I *think* I agree with that but I also believe you always have a choice. You can sacrifice the job of someone who isn't on board or you risk sacrificing lots of jobs. Maybe it's my own rationalization," he says, "but people either have to be with the program or not. There's not time to deal with subversives or people who don't want to be here."

To help managers at Staples get it right the first time, Sargent has put in place the following programs designed to identify and retain team members who fit into the company's culture:

- Promote from within

- Move people around

- Identify rising stars

- Make everyone an owner

- Communicate with your workers

- Make diversity a priority

Promote from Within

"Hiring the wrong people slows a company down," says Sargent, "and we work relentlessly to make sure we're hiring people who will fit our culture. Once we get the right person in the door we focus on getting them trained, fully engaged, and then we begin promoting them as quickly as possible so they'll stay challenged."

Sargent says that Staples will only look outside the company for an executive after an exhaustive companywide internal search fails to produce the right candidate. The company has only used an outside search firm three times in the seven years that he's been the CEO.

Promoting from within pays off in many ways. It creates a career culture that encourages people to stay longer and stretch their skills. It allows managers to select from candidates who are known performers and have proven they can fit in. And most of all it cuts the costs of that long learning curve, an inevitable expense when you hire outsiders. Insiders have tribal knowledge. They understand all it takes to get stuff done—the inner realities, the obstacles, and the intricate web of relationships that are unique to every organization.

Move People Around

"People stay engaged when they're provided new challenges," says Sargent. "The psychological profile of the right Staples candidate is someone who wants a career and wants to grow professionally and financially. We move people into new and different roles as quickly as their development warrants."

Moving people around to new positions, different stores, and new cities and giving successful team members new responsibilities also helps improve productivity. Research shows that people generate their largest productivity improvements in their first year or two in the job. The secret is that on average new people have fresher eyes and have an easier time letting go of old ways and processes that no longer add value.

Identify Rising Stars

Each year Sargent spends three days huddled with his leadership team identifying what the company calls "High Potentials" and "Rising Stars." "It's a very rigorous process that allows us to identify successors for every key role in the company."

Workers with high potential and those who've been designated as rising stars are more likely to remain with an organization when they know their good works have been acknowledged and the company has a future in mind for them. Companies benefit from the exercise because they're always prepared for growth by having a list of people ready to be promoted and take on new responsibilities.

Sargent cites the case of Demos Parneros, Staples's president of U.S. stores, as an example of the importance of identifying rising stars and high potentials. "Demos began as the general manager of one of our stores," says Sargent, "and today serves as the operating head of our largest division." The people who lead Staples's marketing, merchandising, and contract sales are other examples of workers who were identified as future stars and worked their way to the top ranks.

Make Everyone an Owner

Sargent says that the company's reward system of pay for performance and ownership in the company is an essential part of Staples's culture. "Our associates (individual contributors) at the $50,000 level begin receiving restricted stock," he says, "and it scales up from there. Associates at other levels participate in ownership through our 401(k) program where we match their contribution in company stock, and we also offer an ESPP program, which allows workers to purchase company stock at a discount to its market value." Sargent says, "It's vital that the way we reward people matches the interests of the shareholders and that the ownership mentality is constantly reinforced.

"When I became the CEO," Sargent says, "we had about sixty different bonus plans. Today we have two. Everyone in the home office (including Sargent) is compensated based on companywide metrics including earnings per share, sales revenue, return on net assets (RONA),* and customer satisfaction. In our stores," he says, "the management team and hourly associates have bonus goals based on that store's financial performance and customer satisfaction scores. Our results have improved dramatically because everyone is focused on the same goals."

---

*RONA is a measure of financial performance and equals a company's net income divided by its fixed assets and net working capital.

Communicate with Your Workers

Besides Sargent's visits to more than two hundred stores each year, where he has the opportunity to interact with Staples front-line associates, the company also invests considerable resources in communicating with its workers. "Remember the important advice I gave you earlier," Sargent says, "if you don't let people know what's going on, they'll assume that nothing is going on."

Staples created a program called the Breakfast Club, an open forum where all workers can ask questions of the company's leadership; all-associate meetings several times annually called Stake in Staples, and regular director and vice presidential forums to update and solicit feedback. "One of the great parts of our heritage that we've kept," says Sargent, "is regularly gathering our teams together to listen to them and update them."

Make Diversity a Priority

Most companies have finally come to the realization, sometimes reluctantly, that embracing diversity is not only the right thing to do; it makes good business sense to have your company look like its customers. Unfortunately, while many companies talk the talk, they fail to walk the walk and their commitment to diversity is still designated a *special* HR project. Staples has made diversity part of the lifeblood of the company.

As of 2008 women make up nearly half of all associates in the company, and minority associates make up more than one third. Women constitute one third of senior management and minorities make up 10 percent of the company's top leadership. The company is consistently ranked as one of the fifty most diverse companies in the nation and reports on its diversity progress as part of what it calls Staples Soul, the company's corporate responsibility efforts.

Hit the Ground Running Rule 4
Find, Keep, and Grow the Right People

No leader can implement change or run a successful company without the right people. And if you aren't able to *keep* the right people you will never achieve your full economic potential.

- Hire the right people—not warm bodies.
- Promote from within.
- Give people new challenges and move them around.
- Have a program in place to identify rising stars.
- Make everyone an owner.
- Communicate with them or they'll think nothing is happening.
- Look like your customers; make diversity a top priority.

Rule 5: See Through the Fog

Pat Hassey, CEO of Allegheny Technologies Incorporated (ATI), says he learned one of life's most important lessons very early into his first job. "I observed that if you do a good job, people want you. Nobody ever wants you for what you were trained to do; they want you for your ability to get a job done."

Before coming to ATI, Hassey spent his entire career at Alcoa, the same company that hired him out of college and where he ended up as an executive vice president running a $4 billion business group before taking an early retirement at age fifty-seven. When he was asked to become CEO of beleaguered ATI only a few months into his retirement, he was ready to accept the challenge. He told me, "My first total failure was my retirement."

When asked the key to his success at ATI, he offered no hesitation in responding. "It's the job of the CEO to see through the fog and to be a destination expert. People want to know where the company is headed, what their future holds, the opportunities that exist for them, and what their role is going to be. And they don't want to wait forever to find those things out."

ATI

ATI has a distinguished industrial history and has long been an innovator in specialty metals. ATI developed and commercialized stainless steel, and its stainless steel can been seen on New York City's Chrysler Building. Its titanium- and nickel-based alloys were used on the first jet engines and jet-powered airplanes. ATI's zirconium products were used in the first commercial nuclear power plant in the United States. As one of the few significant specialty metals companies, ATI is a *Fortune* 500 producer with $5.5 billion in annual revenues in 2007.

The company's three primary market segments include a flat-rolled products segment (used for tubing, pipes, and applications as diverse as the roof of the world's largest airport terminal in Qatar to flow lines bringing oil from the ocean depths); a high-performance metals segment that includes titanium, zirconium, nickel- and cobalt-based super alloys, and specialty alloys (used in applications from jet engines and airframes to nuclear reactors to biomedical implants and wire for MRI machines); and an engineered products segment that specializes in advanced machining systems, large castings, and alloy steel forgings.

ATI is the result of a 1996 merger of Allegheny Ludlum Corporation and Teledyne, Inc. It would require an entire book to do a postmortem on the events that took place after the two companies combined. Business history has repeatedly proven that successful mergers are as common as purple unicorns. The Allegheny Technologies union was no exception.

Soon after the merger occurred, spin-offs and sales of business units began, and after a little over three years, two operating groups were simultaneously spun off to ATI's shareholders as public companies in their own right.

While a sense of confusion started to reign internally because of leadership issues, outside forces battered the company even harder. The economy went upside down, and the marketplace for essentially all of ATI's products was in a severe slump and was becoming flooded with cheap imports. Finally, in utter frustration, the company developed a stretch business plan (again, conduct about as unusual as those purple unicorns), which insiders say was impossible to achieve under the circumstances. Not surprisingly, several years of consecutive quarterly losses followed. Morale inside the company hit an all-time low.

News stories in the business press painted a picture of a company that was badly broken. By the time Pat Hassey arrived, ATI was losing lots of money, cash was beginning to run low, market share was declining, people were blaming each other for the company's misfortunes, there was very little trust in one another's business judgment, and the only shared glimmer of hope was that perhaps a rebounding economy might help.

Pat Hassey

Pat Hassey's father died following major surgery six months before Pat was born, leaving his mother with a newborn baby boy and a thirteen-month-old daughter. "You can imagine what it must have been like," Hassey says, "with everyone in our highly opinionated and emotional New York, Irish-German family giving her advice and telling her what to do. She finally accepted an invitation from her sister to visit California for a few months, loaded us on a train, and headed west."

Hassey's mother liked California. With the proceeds from his father's insurance, she purchased a modest home in Long Beach, where she raised her children as a stay-at-home mother. When the money ran out, she went to work in the Long Beach school system as a librarian's aide.

"My mother was a strong woman," he says, "although she didn't care much for doctors and hospitals after what happened to my father. She never remarried but committed herself to raising the two of us and being very involved in the community and service organizations. She really believed in hard work and was constantly reminding us that we could achieve whatever we wanted if we really believed we could, but that it was up to us to make it happen."

Other than missing a father he never knew, Hassey recalls a largely idyllic childhood. "My grandmother built a summer house on Lake Erie," he says, "and every year we'd take the train across the country and spend summers in this huge old house with eight bedrooms and every family would have their own room.

"I had a lot of great friends growing up," he adds. "I got A's and B's without studying too much and loved playing intramural baseball. But with more than 3,900 students at Long Beach Wilson High, you had to be a great athlete to be a star.

"My mother got my sister and me involved in one of these social cotillions where they teach manners and ballroom dancing," Hassey says, "and when I was fourteen they hired me as part of the staff." Hassey says he was making a princely wage for the time (1960) of between $5 and $10 an hour.

Hassey enrolled at California State University Long Beach, where he studied business. "I was always fascinated with business," he says, and easily aced his courses in economics, finance, marketing, and sales.

"It was a lot different coming out of college in the 1960s," he says. "When I graduated there were recruiters crawling all over campus trying to hire graduates." After eleven interviews, Pat decided he'd done enough interviewing, canceled the rest of them and, despite offers from IBM, Standard Oil, and Texaco, took a job with Alcoa (the world's largest aluminum producer) because at $630 a month, it was offering to pay him more money than the others.

At twenty-one, Hassey's first job was supposed to be in strategic planning, but when he showed up for work at Alcoa's Vernon

Works, he discovered that plans had changed and he was put in charge of a thirty-one-person transportation office. "It was a good job for me because I got to observe and learn a lot about people," he says. "Many of these people had been there a long time and it was fascinating to figure out who was qualified, who wasn't, which processes helped them in their work, which didn't, and how to build a team.

"The three most important observations I made early on in my career," he notes, "were that most people are loyal and want to do a good job and be successful, that offering a sincere thank you goes a long way, and that a *soft* response is always better than a harsh one.

"The office was right above the company cafeteria," Hassey says, "and everybody either worked in cubicles that were glass from the waist up or in open spaces so everyone could see what everybody else was doing. There was a huge time clock and when that clock struck twelve signaling the beginning of the forty-five-minute lunch break," he adds, "if somebody happened to be walking up the stairs they would have been trampled by the crowd rushing down the stairs to be first in the lunch line."

Hassey reasoned that if most people are loyal and want to do a good job, there was no need for a time clock. "Why subject everyone to rules that were put in place for a few bad apples?" he asked. And so, at the ripe old age of twenty-one, he made his first executive decision and got rid of the time clock.

Hassey learned another lifelong leadership lesson in that cubicle village. The department had a senior invoice checker who would ring a bell every time she found a mistake. "Ding, ding, ding, 'Betty,' the woman would call loud enough for the whole floor to hear," Hassey remembers. "Everyone in the office would know that Betty made a mistake. And Betty was told (with everybody watching) 'Fix it!'" Hassey shakes his head. That was a great lesson in what not to do and changed Hassey's thoughts about the best way for a manager to correct a subordinate's mistakes.

His next couple of jobs involved reporting to people who served Pat as lifelong reminders of the type of manager and leader he hoped to become or never become.

"My next position was as a production planner. My job was to schedule the work and anticipate everything needed to complete it. In order for me to learn as much as I could, my boss had me rotating through several of the production centers in the plant. And while he was a terrific person, all of the production superintendents that I had to work for did not fall into that same category. One was a real dictator," he says, "one of those guys who nobody ever dares question. Besides being a tyrant, he loved going to his boss and showing him all the additional outside work he was responsible for bringing into the company.

"One day I mentioned to him that by the time we did the required special setups and changeovers for the projects he was bringing in, we weren't making a profit. I suggested we should either charge more or stop doing the work," Hassey says. "He got so angry that I'd challenge him that he paid me back by making certain I was the only employee not invited to the big Christmas party at his house."

But Hassey was tenacious and did some further financial analysis that proved the company was indeed losing a few thousand dollars on every outside order the superintendent brought in. "I presented the information to him privately," Hassey says, "he almost blew a gasket. After that he really wanted me out of his department and so I quickly moved on to the extrusion department."

Soon after he arrived there Hassey's boss moved him into a position as a process engineer even though his background was in finance, economics, and marketing. "The process engineer that I worked with wasn't very happy about a twenty-three-year-old kid being sent into his department, but I was excited. He'd been around for thirty years and I figured I could learn a lot from him," he said, "and I was eager to learn."

"Every time I'd ask him 'How do we do this?' or 'Why do we do that?' he'd get upset and snap at me, 'I don't know why you want to know that.' I finally figured out why he wouldn't answer my questions. He couldn't. He really didn't have thirty years of experience," says Hassey. "He had five years of experience six times over, meaning he really *couldn't* answer my questions and to protect himself had built a silo and viewed every question as an attack on his little world.

"These experiences taught me some lessons I've never forgotten," says Hassey. "I promised I'd never let myself get into a position where I'd stop growing," he says, explaining that "everybody has a question, an idea, and an opinion, and if you take the time to listen, you'll end up with a better business. There's no such thing as a dumb question or idea.

"Another thing I learned is that people don't quit companies," he says. "They quit bosses. And the bosses they quit are the ones without integrity. I've worked in many places and for tough bosses and soft bosses. I can work for any kind of boss with one exception: I promised myself I'd never work for someone I couldn't trust. And I came to understand that the best boss becomes a mentor."

Pat quickly moved from one position and one plant to another, earning a reputation in Alcoa as someone who could be trusted, build a team, and deliver a result. When he was twenty-nine he received a phone call asking him to move to Iowa and take over a production unit in one of Alcoa's most important plants. "By that time in my career I'd run fabricating units," he says, "but I hadn't had full P&L (profit and loss) responsibility. Then I was responsible for the Foil Mill at Davenport."

Hassey spent eighteen years at that Iowa plant. Moving from the Foil Mill to works production manager and then, under the mentoring of Sandy Nelson, who Hassey describes as "a great boss and leader," to works manager and then to the head of aerospace sales and marketing for the entire business unit. After Nelson left Alcoa, Hassey was promoted to vice president, Alcoa commercial rolled products, by Paul O'Neill, Alcoa's then CEO and a leader who has achieved near legendary status inside Alcoa. He would become another of Pat's mentors.

After O'Neill retired, the new CEO, Alain Belda, would eventually ask him to head Alcoa Europe. "When Alain sent me to Europe, his marching orders were to make sense out of the company's various holdings across the continent. I decided that the best way to improve the odds for Alcoa's success in Europe was to operate as a single, pan-European company. You have to remember that back in 2000," says Hassey, "there were very few truly pan-European companies," adding that "fierce nationalistic pride prevented it."

"I've learned that the only way to build a team," says Hassey, "is to make sure that everyone understands that as the team succeeds, the individual members succeed. So the first thing I did in Europe was to bring all the country heads together. When the meeting began, I looked at them and said, 'Put your pens down, we'll talk about business later. First, we're going to talk about something more important and that's how we are going to work together and treat each other.'" He spoke to them about the importance of building an environment where mutual trust, respect, and dignity were key. Pat then told the group that from that point forward, their compensation would be dependent on the entire group's performance but, before talking further about business, they were going to talk about mutual trust, respect, and dignity.

Pat Hassey's Team Rules

One of Hassey's strong guiding principles is that until employees believe that their boss cares about their personal well-being as much as the well-being of the company, they won't trust him and won't be willing to become committed and engaged in what the business is trying to achieve. "You have to treat people fairly," he says, "with dignity, by listening, and valuing each person as an individual. Otherwise it's impossible to build a team."

Hassey's definition of a team is a group of people who've come together to achieve a common purpose. Members of a Hassey-led team have to agree to the following principles:

- Everyone will always be treated with respect and dignity.

- Everyone will always operate with the highest level of integrity.

- People will be valued as individuals.

- Everyone will have a voice and be heard.

- There will be no finger pointing, posturing, or posing.

- People will be fairly compensated as team contributors.

- Everyone will work collaboratively to achieve the plan.

- People will be recognized when they do well.

- Everyone agrees to do the best job they can.

- Everyone is committed to helping out other team members.

- If someone is doing poorly, then somebody else will pitch in.

Following Hassey's successful run as president of Alcoa's European holdings, he returned to the United States and headed a $4 billion business group before retiring at fifty-seven. "My separation from Alcoa was congenial," he says, "but the landscape changed after Paul O'Neill retired. The new CEO and I didn't see eye to eye on the direction the company was moving."

Pat's retirement lasted only long enough to take his wife on the Alaskan cruise he'd been promising her for forty years. But even before the boat had left the port, he was approached by former Alcoa President and ATI board member Fred Fetterolf about becoming a consultant and possibly joining the ATI board. "It turns out," he says with a big grin, "that the consulting assignment and possible board membership were actually friendly ruses designed by the then ATI chairman, Bob Bozzone, whom I had also met in my Alcoa days, so that I'd see how much potential the company had and would want the CEO's job."

Building His Team

Hassey says (and everyone we interviewed at ATI agreed) that when he became CEO the company was in "tough shape." His first goal was to stop any bleeding and get everything back on track. "Everybody," says Hassey, "was looking for someone to help pull them out of the hole they were in."

But when Hassey took charge, he saw something that many new bosses miss. Anytime a company is hemorrhaging, it's certain that some, or many, people have been wounded. So to get the organization back to health he decided not only to stop the bleeding but also to address the needs of the injured.

"Three of the top four company executives had been contenders for the position of CEO," he says, "and I had to deal with those disappointed people first." Hassey got them all together and told them, "I'm not going to fire anyone. Everybody has a job." He then explained that when the board offered him the CEO's position, they'd already ruled out hiring any of the internal candidates and had retained an executive search firm. "I told them," Hassey says, "that if one of them had still been a viable candidate, I would have turned the job down."

Hassey probably surprised them even more with what he said

next. He told each of these four executives, the COO, CFO, general counsel, and chief technical officer, that they would receive equal salaries. This meant substantial raises for three of the four executives, but all of their jobs were going to change significantly.

"I explained to them that while each of them would be making the same amount of money, stock options were a thing of the past but that there would be a significant bonus pool of cash to be divided equally if the company performed well and met predetermined stretch financial goals over a three-year period. We knew it would be a tough job but success could mean several million dollars for each member of the team. Some of the executives expressed surprise at the potential value of the pay packages," Hassey says.

"Until people believe that you're as interested in their personal well-being as you are in the well-being of the company, they won't get on the team. These were all talented and good people and I needed to keep them in the company," he explains. "They'd been here a long time and through no major missteps taken by them, the company was about to sink. They could have jumped ship, so I wanted them to understand clearly that I needed and would reward their help."

But Hassey is not a big spender. His plan included getting more productivity out of every dollar in executive compensation. "I told them we didn't have money to spend hiring lots of new people and that we didn't need a big crowd running around the headquarters, so that meant that each of their jobs was going to expand."

Hassey increased the responsibilities of the general counsel and corporate secretary to include head of HR and chief compliance officer. He told the COO he didn't want a reporting step between the CEO and the operating presidents and that while the role of COO was being eliminated, he'd become chief engineer, head of the company's collective bargaining committee, take over the engineered products segment, and head up capital spending for the company. The CFO was given six jobs, including purchasing, IT, and responsibility for the pension fund. The chief technical officer became the head of the company's international group, government relations, and joint ventures.

Hassey, of course, asked for their help. "The final thing I told them," says Hassey, "is that I needed each of them to become my counselor." Hassey promised that no decision would be made until each had voiced his or her opinion and everyone knew the whole story. "Once we make a decision together," Hassey told them, "everyone needs to support it and everyone has to be seen as supporting it. Without that sort of unified effort, things won't work."

Once Hassey's core executives were in place, he formed and led an executive committee composed of the four people mentioned previously and the presidents of the company's four key operating units. The group meets regularly to discuss key issues and make the kind of unified decisions Pat feels are critical.

"I've found that when you listen to lots of different voices and viewpoints that you'll get very close to the right decision and to what you should be doing," says Hassey, adding, "but don't confuse a decision made after listening to lots of people with a *compromise* decision." Hassey says he's not a fan of compromise decisions that try to satisfy everyone. "Usually, when you get to a compromise, you've lost something," he explains. "You seek input, carefully consider everything you've heard, and then make the call," adding that "the right decision has generally become obvious by that point."

Seeing Through the Fog

"Even though it's often foggy out there," Hassey says, "I don't buy not being able to look out and see a quarter, one, two, or even three years ahead. You consider what's happening in the world, in your business, figure out where the opportunities are, what the challenges are, and try to connect the dots to forecast the future. People want to know where they're being asked to go, how the company is going to get there, the things that need to be done, and the role they're going to play."

Hassey is spot on. It is essential for leaders to be anticipating as far as they can—recognizing problems and opportunities before they are obvious, seeing new paths to exploit, having the courage to try them, measure their results, and the maturity to adapt. But many executives are passive. They wait for all uncertainty to clear and rely on their ability to deal with things after they hit their desk.

In fact, when Fuld and Company surveyed 140 corporate strategists, 97 percent said their companies lacked any early warning system to help them anticipate changing demand for what they sell, changing customer requirements, or changing market conditions. Yet two thirds of these same companies had been unhappily surprised by something huge—for example, new competitors "eating their lunch," huge spikes in the cost of materials that meant they could no longer compete, and changed economic conditions that rendered them irrelevant over and over during the previous five years. Still these organizations remained passive.

As Hassey (with the help of his team) looked through the fog, they came to several conclusions about their business. They believed that:

- The global capital goods* market would remain strong far into the future.

- The aerospace industry was in the early stages of a "super" build cycle.

---

*Capital goods are things produced by a company to be used in the manufacturing of a product for another end purchaser, for example, a specialty metal that a general contractor purchases from Allegheny to build a roof for his customer.

- Developing economies would have a huge appetite for electrical energy.

- The world was in the early stages of a massive infrastructure build.

Lots of things at ATI required repair, but Hassey isn't a fan of the word F-I-X. "When you have to fix something," he says, "you're implying that it's badly broken and in the long term nobody will want to work for or buy stock in a company that's being fixed." Hassey says that a more appropriate description of what occurred at ATI was transformation. "We had an opportunity here to become the 'world's best specialty metals company' and that was the story we built for our employees and for Wall Street."

Once Hassey and his team knew where the real potential existed, understood what they wanted the company to become, and had the players in place (including having preserved the institutional knowledge), they were ready to hit the ground running.

The Transformation

Hassey didn't have the luxury of time as he assessed how to transform ATI into the company he believed it could be. There was enough cash on hand to power the company for a period of time. Then the well could run dry. Hassey and his team knew six things had to happen quickly if the company's fortunes were going to be reversed and ATI was to become the world's best specialty metals company. They had to:

- Reduce operating expenses

- Stop the bleeding

- Sign a new union contract

- Align all divisions with the markets they were going after

- Become a price leader instead of a price follower

- Improve the balance sheet and cash liquidity

Reduce Operating Expenses

Too often a new CEO who decides that cost cutting is required begins slashing costs at the bottom of the organization. Pat Hassey started at the top.

"We had people scattered all over PPG Place, which is where our corporate center is physically located," says Hassey, "so I decided we'd put everyone on one floor. It'd save us money and make communication more efficient, too. See that reception area out there?" he says, pointing his finger. "Believe it or not, that used to be part of the CEO's office. Next door was a huge conference room just for this office. I told people, 'I don't need a lounge area and a private conference room. I just need a table to work on.'" The conference room was made into an office for one of the executives. While he was at it, he asked to have the CEO's private bathroom, which had been remodeled by a predecessor, closed. "Why in the world would I need a private bathroom?" he asks.

When people see a CEO lead by example, they begin to follow suit. And that's what happened at ATI. Harkening back to one of Hassey's basic beliefs that people instinctively want to do the right thing, suddenly people were treating the company's financial resources as their own and enthusiastically embraced the cost-cutting measures.

Stop the Bleeding

Besides reducing operating expenses, Pat also called on one of the earliest business lessons he learned at Alcoa from the dictatorial production superintendent who bragged to his superiors about all the outside business he was bringing in—most of which proved to be a money-losing proposition. "We had to figure our where we made money, so we began a rigorous examination of everything we did, asking the most basic of business questions, 'Is this profitable?'" Hassey says. Every product the company manufactured, by segment, product form, and customer, was examined with surprising results.

"We discovered we had some bad customers," he says, "and we had to fire them." Hassey argues that a company mustn't keep unprofitable customers solely for the sake of the revenue they create. "Get rid of bad and unprofitable customers and your earnings will increase.

"A big mistake that many executives make," says Hassey, "is looking only at the top line number and assuming that all revenue is good revenue. That's simply not true. Better managers look at the numbers behind the big number. The best managers want to know how the underlying numbers were generated."

Sign a New Union Contract

"Our union contracts were obsolete and not reflective of the realities in the metals business," says Hassey. "We had to renegotiate them and have them make sense for everyone, including the union workers."

When discussing unions, most CEOs roll their eyes and begin hurling expletives across the room and blaming all their problems on the unions. Not Pat Hassey. "My belief," Hassey says, "is to have a collaborative relationship with the unions or you'll end up spending all your time fighting and life is too short for that. Our union members are our manufacturing experts, we acknowledge them for their skills and talents, and I care as much about their well-being as I do my own, but that doesn't necessarily make them process experts also.

"When we occasionally disagree with the unions (outside the normal, multiyear contract negotiations)," he says, "it is over our never ending quest for simplification. When we began negotiating our contract, the union pointed out that our plants and workers were the best in the world and they were so flexible they were capable of producing the same product twenty-seven different ways. I told them I didn't want to be able to produce a product twenty-seven different ways. I wanted to do it one way, the best way, and do it that way every time.

"I'd rather have a unionized plant in the United States any day," he says, citing one of ATI's plants in Midland, Pennsylvania, "where our fifty-two union workers, each earning more than $100,000 annually, including full benefits, can produce 300,000 tons of stainless steel a year, competing with a plant in China with 2,000 people making 70 cents an hour. It's better for our economy," he adds, revealing his fierce patriotism, "and it's better for America."

Another example of Hassey's commitment to the financial well-being of everyone is the company's pension plan; when he took over, the plan was underfunded by more than $400 million. As of the end of 2007 it was funded at 111 percent of the required amount.

Align All Divisions

It is one thing to look through the fog and select where you want to take a company, but it's another thing to get all the operating divisions and thousands of people pointed in the same direction. That's where most leaders fall short. They talk a good game, pontificate about where they're headed, and then they're unable to execute.

Hassey's secret weapons were the company's top leaders (who stood to earn a lot of money if it all worked); a new union contract, which made the company competitive and offered flexibility; and a consensus belief that this leader cared as much about the company and them as he did himself.

Stop Being a Price Follower

Anyone who knows anything about sales will agree that when the only thing you have to talk about with a potential buyer is price, there's only one direction for the price to go—and that's down. Furthermore, conventional wisdom dictates that when you're selling a commodity, there's nothing other than price to talk about. After all, the definition of commodity is a good, product, or service whose price is set by the marketplace based on supply and demand. Wheat, copper, oil, apples, and many metals are all commodities.

Before Hassey's arrival, ATI was firmly in the commodities business; it was desperate for cash, selling many products based essentially on price, and was often being beaten by lower-priced rivals. On the commodities side, this left ATI with few options other than lowering its prices even further if it wanted the business.

All of that changed when Hassey took the helm. "Just because we make commodities doesn't mean we're in the commodities business," he says. "A company only ends up in the commodity business if their products are exactly like their competitors without any discernible differences between them."

"The first thing we had to do," he says, "was understand and start believing that we were different and better than our competitors. We offer a constant stream of new alloys and products needed by our customers, stellar service, geopolitical stability, and the best engineering in the business. Each of those things taken alone means little, but added together, they mean a lot."

To demonstrate how ATI doesn't sell commodities, Hassey offered the following example. "Imagine you're an end user who needs titanium, nickel-based alloy plate or hydraulic tubing. Would you want to buy your titanium from an unstable region with unpredictable leaders (you know who and where) who have a history of holding customers hostage for political or economic leverage? Or would you prefer," he asks, "to deal with one company and know that for a little more, you're going to get your delivery on time, that it will be faultlessly engineered, and that your supplier will do whatever it takes to make your life easier and better?"

Hassey believes ATI's $2.5 billion long-term agreement with Boeing to supply titanium for airplanes, particularly the new 787 Dreamliner, goes a long way in answering these questions. Impressively, ATI has a near 100 percent delivery record at Boeing.

By packaging the specialty metals it sells the same way that a car dealer offers package A or package B on accessories, ATI was able to begin moving out of the commodities business and quickly began increasing margins. "There are two ways to make a profit," says Hassey, "cut your costs or increase the margins on what you're selling." In the ideal situation, he says, "you do both."

Raise Some Money

Hassey's next step was to inject some operating capital. "I really don't like the word *story*," he says, "but when you're going out to raise money you'd better have a good one. And by that time we had a great story to tell about having the right management, the right destination, a union contract buttoned down, the right strategy in place and our transformation was underway."

Hassey and his team embarked on a two-week road show calling on investors, some of whom had previously been ATI shareholders and many who had never owned ATI stock. They were offering 10 million shares of stock at $17.50. By the end of the trip, ATI had sold 13 million shares (the maximum allowed) raising $230 million.

Get Some Results

Hassey's efforts to hit the ground running worked.

"We started making some money in 2004, my first full year as CEO. The magic," he says, "is watching what happens to people when they see things begin to work. They want more and they want to perform even better."

Everyone who bought those ATI shares at $17.50 made out very well. During Hassey's tenure, revenues have tripled and net income has risen from a loss to nearly three quarters of a billion dollars in 2007. One hundred dollars invested in ATI's shares in 2001 is now worth $1,200 while the stock of ATI's peers is worth $350.

Hit the Ground Running Rule 5
See Through the Fog

Pat Hassey says that an effective leader must be the destination expert. He or she must effectively communicate where the organization is headed and the role that people will play, and address the all important . . . *What's in it for me?*

The first steps at Allegheny were pretty obvious—getting back on track by stopping the bleeding, healing the wounded, and then making the current operations efficient and effective. But three first steps weren't going to take ATI to the destination Hassey had in mind. He saw a truly transformed ATI, creating a different business model so the company could have a different and much more successful future. Those steps weren't as obvious.

Rule 5: See Through the Fog

Anytime you are forecasting the future, you are going to need to see through the fog of uncertainty. Hassey argues that seeing through the fog isn't that difficult if you'll be *ruthlessly* honest and answer the following questions:

- What's really happening in the world (your markets)? What trends or needs are becoming obvious and are likely to be long rather than short term?
- What are the capabilities (or potential capabilities) of your company that would allow you to service these developing trends or needs?
- Do you have the team and the knowledge in place that will allow you to service these developing trends or needs?
- Do you have or can you find the financial resources to service these developing trends or needs?

Once you've connected the dots, your destination(s) will become obvious.

Rule 6: Drive a Stake in the Ground

Our words and deeds—even those we consider inconsequential at the time—frequently make lifelong impressions on other people. Mike McCallister, CEO of Humana, vividly recalls two events that happened early in the thirty-five years he's spent with the company.

"I was in my first job out of college working in a small Louisiana hospital for Humana and something made a real impact on me," he says. "The administrator of the hospital took the time to know the first name of everyone on staff, including the guy who mopped the floors, and he always took the time to greet everyone by name and treat them with incredible respect." Later, McCallister saw the big payoff for this simple effort. He frequently observed the administrator deal with potentially big problems with ease simply because people believed he was interested in and cared about them.

"And the opposite of caring about people enough to learn their names," McCallister says, "was brought home to me at a regional meeting I went to a few years later with a senior executive in the company. The region was having a bad year, and this guy got up in front of all his hospital CEOs and ranted and raved about how awful we were doing. 'A lot of you aren't going to be here next year!' he threatened. The next day he called me and said, 'How'd I do?' 'Terrible,' I told him. He was shocked and asked why. 'A few of us will be leaving, no doubt,' I said, 'but you made every single one of us hang our heads and feel like giving up.' Right then and there I vowed to myself that no matter what kind of leadership position I was in or what the business circumstances were, I would never be a bully."

McCallister is an understated, every-word-counts kind of guy who'd rather observe a situation before talking about it. He's fiercely independent, doesn't take himself too seriously, and it's easy to imagine knocking back a few beers and arguing sports with him. "I can't say I've ever had any heroes," he says, "but if you keep your eyes open and observe people it's not *too hard* to figure who you want to be like and who you don't."

Through his observation over the years, McCallister picked up on many patterns of effective and ineffective leadership behavior, and has since used what he learned in both business and everyday life. Most important he's grasped the key lesson that's led directly to his success in running a variety of organizations—hospitals, health plans, and now the entire company—within the Humana system: If you want to hit the ground running and make great things happen you need to drive a stake in the ground.

Humana

Humana was founded in 1961 by David Jones and Wendell Cherry, two young lawyers in Louisville, Kentucky, who joined four other friends and put up $1,000 each to open a nursing home called Heritage House. By 1968, the company had changed its name to Extendicare, owned seven nursing homes, and went public to raise money for further expansion. With some of the proceeds from their IPO they purchased a hospital that was under construction in Huntsville, Alabama.

A few years later, after purchasing another ten hospitals, even though they'd become the nation's largest operator of nursing homes, they sold them off to concentrate on buying, building, and operating hospitals. In 1974 they changed the company name to Humana and were soon building and opening a new hospital every month and gobbling up their competitors. By the early 1980s they owned more than eighty hospitals in the United States and Europe and had become the world's largest hospital company.

Until Humana started the wave of consolidation and privatization that eventually became the new face of medical care, most American hospitals were guided by local businessmen who served as the board of directors and run by the doctors who admitted patients to the hospital. At the time, even critics of "chain" hospitals recognized the huge potential efficiencies and increases in productivity that centralized buying and standardized policies and procedures could bring to the industry.

The company was widely acknowledged as an innovative operator of hospitals and pioneered the quantitative measurement of hospital quality and patient care and invented a new emergency room design that became the industry norm. Humana also created an innovative program that designated a leading Humana hospital in many regions of the country as a "Center of Excellence" for important medical specialties that provided patients everywhere access to specialized medical care.

As Humana's leadership team members looked through the fog they realized that dramatic improvements in health care would eventually take a toll on their hospital business in the form of more outpatient procedures and fewer hospital admissions. So in 1984 they created and began offering managed-care insurance products called Humana Care Plus. They reasoned that if revenues from hospital admissions were likely to decline, they could replace the lost revenue with insurance premiums and possibly even exert some control over both sides of the equation.

But all was not ideal. The company increasingly appeared to be working at cross-purposes. On the one hand, physicians were encouraged to fill Humana hospitals. On the other hand, the insurance segment worked hard to obtain favorable contracts from network doctors to keep down costs and member premiums. The internal stresses eventually resulted in the company deciding in 1993 to split in two, with the hospitals establishing a separate existence as Galen Healthcare.

Following the separation, Humana put the pedal to the metal in the insurance business the same way it had done in hospitals and began rapidly growing the company organically and through acquisitions. With $25 billion in annual revenues and 26,000 workers and associates the company provides health benefits to more than eleven million health-plan members and has become one of the nation's largest and most innovative health insurance companies.

Mike McCallister

Countless articles and books would have you believe that all highly successful, high-profile CEOs have ruthless ambition in their DNA and that every career move they ever made was calculated in preparation for a well-planned ascension to a top job.

I guess they never met Mike McCallister.

"Much of what's happened in my career has been serendipitous," he says, adding, "there was never a plan, just a lot of fortunate things that happened by accident."

McCallister grew up the oldest child in a family of six. He had two brothers, a sister, and parents who spent their entire careers working for AT&T. They lived in Indianapolis until he finished the eighth grade and then moved to Louisiana, where McCallister went to high school in Shreveport and to college at Louisiana Tech in Ruston. His childhood was typical of that era, filled with memories of snow and Catholic school in Indianapolis, playing basketball and baseball with his friends. He remembers having the freedom to take off in the morning on his bicycle and not return home till dark without anyone worrying about him. "We were free to do anything,"

McCallister reflects, "with a just a few rules like 'Tell us when you'll be back.'" McCallister credits this "incredible freedom" to manage himself within a few simple boundaries with inspiring both his leadership style and his strategy for improving health care.

McCallister says he never gave a moment's thought about what he wanted to do when he grew up. "In high school I started working and never stopped, including lots of menial jobs like pumping gas. One summer I worked as a roofer and after being up on a roof all day in 100 degree heat and 100 percent humidity I remember thinking, 'If this is what real work is all about I don't have any interest in it.' Those menial jobs didn't help me figure out what I wanted to be but," he says, "they sure helped me figure out what I didn't want to be."

Though he remains very close with his family McCallister has been on his own financially since the day he left for college. "We never really talked about it," he says. "It was simply understood that once I left I'd take care of myself, make my own money, and pay my own way." Throughout college he lived year round near the campus, worked as a picture framer, partied a lot, and hung with what he calls an artsy crowd.

After high school, McCallister was admitted to an engineering program at Louisiana Tech. But he decided after a year that engineering was a lot like roofing—something he didn't want to pursue. "There was no way I was going to survive any more calculus or the other courses required to be an engineer," he says. He realized he had to adapt to the situation and practice flexibility with the resources at hand. "So one day I went to the placement office and asked the people there to tell me what companies were looking for when they recruited on campus. The counselor told me they came looking for engineers because Louisiana Tech is a highly regarded engineering school."

"I asked her, 'What else?'"

"She said they also recruited accountants."

"I said, 'Done deal,' and changed my major on the spot."

As he neared graduation, recruiters began visiting campus and McCallister started interviewing with lots of companies including oil and gas companies, accounting firms, and paper mills. "I've always believed," he says, "that if you get into something you don't like you can make a change. I wasn't looking for a lifetime career. I was just going for the next round and hopefully that meant an interesting job, decent pay, and a town I was willing to live in." He realized that at this stage in life, the ability to be flexible and adapt to different environments was valuable. Little did he know he was about to embark on a thirty-four-year journey with the same company.

Due to a last-minute opening in his interviewing schedule he had time to interview with Extendicare, a small company he'd never heard of. "I asked the interviewer what Extendicare did and he said they weren't Extendicare anymore that they'd changed their name to Humana and they owned hospitals. I'd never thought about a job in the health-care industry," he says, "but thought it was interesting and they offered me a job. So, remarkably, my career in health care was launched on the back of an accident. Serendipity." Humana, already in a period of huge growth, was recruiting aggressively to fill its management pipeline and sent McCallister to Springhill, Louisiana, a tiny town on the Louisiana/Arkansas border with a population of 5,439 people.

"The company didn't really tell me what my job was going to be," says McCallister. "I knew it was a finance position, but that was about it. When I got there, the hospital didn't know what to do with me because I'd been hired by corporate and delivered to them. They didn't even know there'd been a job opening."

Springhill Medical Center, the small rural hospital where McCallister was sent, found him a vacant office with a green metal desk, a single four-drawer filing cabinet, an old ten-key calculator, dropped a thick stack of green bar paper on his desk, and told him to go to work on the budget for the next year.

"It was unbelievable," says McCallister. "I didn't know anything at all about hospitals and I was being asked to do the next year's budget." But rather than stay intimidated, McCallister did something he's successfully repeated throughout this career—he learned how the business works, by watching, listening, and asking the right questions.

"I really believe that you can learn what you need to know about any business and what makes it tick," he says, "by just paying attention and figuring out where your business is going to come from and who your key clients are. Hospitals, even small ones, are enormously complicated places. In addition to the normal complexities that come with running any business you also have a medical staff that wields an uncontrollably huge impact and influence on your customers." It was McCallister's conclusion that the key clients of a hospital weren't the patients but the doctors who admitted the patients. "The fact is," he says, "patients can't admit themselves. They come from doctors. And if doctors don't admit patients to your hospital you're out of business."

McCallister quickly decided he liked the hospital business. "I found it fascinating. It was a great place with wonderful people," he says, "all of whom were committed to helping people get well."

He had worked for Humana for only a month when a regional vice president visited the hospital. In the course of conversation with McCallister, he asked the recent graduate where he envisioned his career. Serendipity had introduced him to the health-care industry, but by now he had a clear idea of what he wanted to do with the rest of his life. "I told him that I wanted to run a hospital." McCallister chuckles when he recalls the conversation and says, "Humana was growing very fast in those days and wasn't quite as disciplined from a human-capital perspective as we are now. As a result, the response was, 'OK, let's target your career that way then.'"

Two years later McCallister got a call from the home office telling him there was an opening for an acting administrator in Many,

Louisiana, at another small rural hospital and asking him if he was interested in the job. "Because of my age, they told me I wouldn't be getting a raise [he was making $13,000 a year]. I would only be acting administrator and they wouldn't pay my moving expenses. I immediately said yes." So at the age of twenty-four, McCallister loaded up his car and drove to Many for his first job running a hospital. He has been running businesses ever since.

"The first day I was there," he says, "Frances Hopkins, a wonderful woman and natural leader who was the hospital's controller, came in, introduced herself, sat down, smiled, and said, 'Honey, don't you worry about running a hospital; I'll show you how to do it,' and she did." She served as his mentor, spending several hours daily teaching him how to manage a hospital and freeing his schedule to build relationships with the doctors.

While working in Many, McCallister quickly debunked a big piece of misguided conventional wisdom—that the person in charge should earn the biggest paycheck. "The nurses, doctors, pharmacists, virtually everybody in the hospital," he says, "were making a lot more than I was and that was okay because it taught me a lot about compensating people for the jobs they do and the value they create. I was on a learning curve. They weren't."

His next hospital, in Jackson, Mississippi, was a mere resting stop in McCallister's career while Humana pondered his next destination. This hospital, more than three times the size of the last hospital he ran, was actually easier to administer. Thus, his next lesson: "It's not entirely true that large enterprises are more difficult to manage. The bigger the business, the easier it can be because you have more resources available. If you're running a small hospital and two nurses call in sick and they're your entire shift, you're toast. When you're running a small business you're always close to the edge," he concludes, "while bigger businesses have resources for almost anything that can happen."

In 1978, Humana completed the hostile takeover of a much

larger company on the West Coast and wanted to put its own people and culture into the hospitals there. McCallister was offered a position as an assistant administrator, but he said he'd already been there, done that, and didn't want to take a step backward. As a compromise he became chief administrator of a small Los Angeles hospital and associate administrator at a larger one down the street where the boss was out on sick leave.

While leading those first hospitals in California, McCallister learned another important lesson he's never forgotten. "I was running back and forth between the two," he says. "The larger one was undergoing expansion and adding beds, and the company planned on closing the smaller one when the additions were complete. The small hospital was losing tons of money and there wasn't anything I could do to turn it around because everyone knew it was on its way to being closed.

"I kept asking people why we were keeping the small hospital open and losing money when there were plenty of empty beds a few miles away and everyone kept telling me that the state of California required us to keep it open. The more I thought about it," he says, "the more I thought that their answers were too stupid to be right." McCallister dug a little deeper, learned there was no requirement that the hospital be kept open and in the process learned a lesson. "When your gut is telling you that something you're hearing doesn't add up—even if it is coming from so-called experts—validate it yourself."

As Humana continued moving McCallister around the country, the hospitals kept getting bigger and the challenges more complex. By the time he was in his early thirties he'd become known as one of the company's turnaround specialists, and he'd figured out a few additional lessons that allowed him to hit the ground running at each new hospital.

Don't Be Intimidated: You Are the Authority

One insight into McCallister's fiercely egalitarian nature is that he's always called doctors by their first names. "I was young when I started running my first hospital," he says, "but I quickly realized that the nature of the hospital business, what makes it so difficult and complex, is that physicians who are not employed by the hospital have a huge influence over its success or failure. So it was important from the beginning to be viewed as a peer by the doctors. If I'd started fawning over them and addressing them all as 'Doctor,' they'd have had a big advantage over me."

He recalls gathering around a long conference table with a group of doctors in their lab coats, name tags, and half-moon glasses, analyzing the potential purchase of a cardiac catheterization lab (a project requiring a multimillion dollar investment), when one of the physicians looked him up and down and said, "Why are we even talking to you? We need to talk with someone from Humana Corporate who has authority to make a decision."

No professional wants to waste his time. He wants to know who's in charge and talk only to him or her. But with today's matrixed management and many layers of bureaucracy at even the best companies, knowing who's in charge can be confusing. McCallister always quickly eliminated any confusion.

"My operating model from day one was that *I* was running the hospital and responsible for the final decision," says McCallister. "I never let anyone know when I needed to get approval from a higher up because that would have diminished my authority and my effectiveness."

So McCallister looked straight at the doctor, smiled his biggest smile, and told him, "Joel, you're clueless as to what I can approve or not approve. But let's assume for a moment you're right and that I need to get the approval of someone else. If you go around my back," he told the doctor, "the first thing they'll do when they finish talking with you is call me, ask me what I think. In other words, without me it's dead, and with me it has a chance. So maybe I have the power to say yes and maybe I don't, but I certainly have the power to say no." The doctor stared back, mumbled a quiet okay, and was always more collegial from then on. Although McCallister did not have an absolute say at the time, he asserted the power he did have—the power to say no—and gained the result he wanted.

McCallister believes managers spend too much time whining about not having direct day-to-day control over such staff functions as HR, purchasing, marketing, and legal departments. "I constantly watch people struggle with the issue of centralized services," he says, "especially in matrix organizations. They're so busy driving themselves crazy because they don't have their own lawyer, HR person, or purchasing department and pointing fingers of blame that they don't get anything done. My attitude always was," he says, "great, you folks take care of all that unimportant stuff and I'll do the things that are vital, like making sure the doctors are happy and admitting patients, keeping people motivated, and making sure everyone is moving in the same direction. I never worried over who wrote the contracts or bought the toilet paper.

"I've always believed," he continues, "that if you're going to ask people to look at you as a leader and follow you that you have to take the responsibility and authority for *everything*, even if it isn't your idea. The minute people think the decision is coming from somewhere else, you're finished."

Get It Out in the Open

McCallister believes one of the reasons many companies can't hit the ground running and gain any traction is because the real issues aren't moved into the open and tackled head-on. "One of the hospitals I took over in southern California was in bad shape and in a real catch-22 situation," he recalls. "It was losing money and needed new equipment, but the company wouldn't put any money in until it started being profitable and doctors wouldn't admit any more patients until they got the new equipment they wanted."

McCallister says he worked the doctors relentlessly, spending the first ninety minutes of each day with them in the doctors' lounge trying to get them to admit more patients, to no avail. Finally, he took the doctors away for a two-day off-site at an upscale resort. On the first day they played golf and relaxed, but on the morning of the second day, he gathered the doctors, excused the kitchen staff, closed the doors, and gave them this inspired pitch.

"Here's the deal," he told the doctors. "The company doesn't think very much of this hospital and I don't think you guys care either because you're not supporting the place. I can't get you the equipment you need until we show an improvement and you won't admit more patients until I do. So what would you like me to do?"

With dead silence in the room, he continued, "If you'll agree that for the next sixty days you'll admit every patient to this hospital that makes sense for us to handle, I promise I'll have the company step up and get you the equipment you want. Otherwise," he said, "I'm going to call it a day, go get a job someplace else, and you guys can do whatever you want."

Conventional wisdom underestimates the cooperative nature and the intelligence of most people. That's one reason the conventional manager doesn't let employees see the P&L or let suppliers look behind the facade at the true state of the business. But McCallister believes in people and trusts that when they have the right information, they'll do the right thing. So he believes in getting things out in the open.

The doctors proved McCallister's instincts were right; they told him they'd do it. And McCallister says, "Business started booming and the capital equipment began rolling in. Each time a new piece of equipment arrived I'd send a note to every doctor so they'd know I'd made good on my promise."

Pay Attention to the Right Details

Hospitals pay close attention to how many patients doctors are admitting, and each one wants to make certain they're getting their share because most physicians and physician groups maintain admitting privileges at several hospitals.

"Our hospital staffs would always get excited when a doctor had a high level of admissions," McCallister says, "and they'd all be ready to celebrate and say, 'Oh look, Dr. X has twenty patients in the hospital today.' The reality is that while Dr. Y only had four patients in the hospital because of the procedures and resources used, his patients were far more profitable than Dr. X's.

"If you want to be an effective manager and leader," he says, "you have to figure out what really matters and pay close attention, not to all the details, just the right ones. Identify the centers of influence within the business and make certain the leaders there are also attentive to the right details." McCallister adds, "I've been fortunate to have been around a handful of people during my career who mastered the art of being well grounded, were blessed with good common sense, did their homework, understood the numbers, and paid attention to the right details without losing sight of the big picture."

Let People See That Something Positive Is Happening

When a new boss shows up, workers want to know that things will change and improve. Unless management takes steps to communicate that something positive is going to happen, employees will assume the worst. "If you want to be successful immediately present yourself as an agent of positive change," says McCallister.

McCallister's first order of business when taking over a new hospital was to have the maintenance crew start painting something very visible in the hospital, explaining that painters at work and the smell of paint would signal that some kind of change was taking place. Next, he'd begin walking the parking lot looking for and pointing out litter to be removed. "It didn't take very long," he says, "for everyone to start beating their drums, signaling that change had arrived.

"One of the other things I'd routinely do after taking over a hospital," he says, "was gather a small group of people and go through it floor by floor tearing down all the old paper signs." There were always scores of paper signs taped to walls, yellowed and curled on the edges, that cheapened the look and feel of the hospital. "My attitude is that if a place looks like a dump, people are going to think and act like it's a dump." While admitting that some of the things he'd do simply to send a signal, McCallister (who continues to tear down paper signs whenever he sees them) says, "It never hurts and almost always helps to get and keep people thinking that change is about to take place."

After the walls had been painted and the hospital cleaned up, McCallister would lead his team in a discussion of the fact that it was more expensive to stay in hospitals than five-star hotels and that perhaps they should start treating their patients like welcome guests. This led to another of his trademarks. Each morning, patients would receive a flower on their breakfast tray along with a complimentary newspaper and McCallister's business card; attached was a note encouraging patients to call his extension for a quick resolution if there was a problem any time during their stay.

"You have to constantly search for ways to let people know that things are going to change and that they are going to be better," McCallister stresses.

The Top Job: Reinventing Humana

McCallister continued fixing and running hospitals until he joined the insurance side of Humana as a result of the company's 1993 split. "It was kind of like picking sides for softball teams," he recalls, "The guy on the hospital side got a pick and then the guy on the insurance side would have his turn." Soon McCallister was picked to run all of Humana's insurance operations in San Antonio, Texas. After four years in Texas he was summoned to Louisville, where he served as one of two division presidents responsible for running half the company.

"It was a crazy time," McCallister says. "I'd been here only a few days when the COO left and the next few years are a blur of one reorganization and CEO change after another." In 1997 he was promoted to senior vice president, putting him in charge of all the company's health plans. The next year a big merger failed when the suitor announced a surprise earnings charge, another CEO left, and McCallister says he thought it was time for him to leave too.

"I wasn't sure I was going to stay," he says. "Being in the corporate office was too far away from the action. Because I'd been running my own business units for more than twenty-five years, I didn't really enjoy reporting to a boss on a day-to-day basis and frankly didn't think I'd last long." Following a transitional stint as part of a three-person office of the chairman, McCallister put up his hand and said, "I think I can run this company and want to be considered." After landing the CEO position a few months later, McCallister was in his element as the sole authority figure. "Then it became fun again because I was back in the top leadership position and could hopefully make a positive difference."

Now it was 2000, seven years after the split, and the new Humana was in chaos. "Our financial performance was a mess," he says. "There was no strategy, our reputation was poor, and nobody expected very much from us." McCallister says the company's poor situation also provided him and his team a unique opportunity. "Because expectations were low," he says, "we had breathing room— time to ask ourselves what business we were in, where we wanted to go, and what we wanted to be," adding, "most companies never have that strategic luxury."

Before McCallister could address where he wanted to take the company, he had some cleanup to do. "Some people will disagree," says McCallister, "but I don't think turnaround work is very hard." The company had made acquisitions that weren't doing well, had written some bad business that was costing them money, and didn't have a lot of cash. "During a turnaround you do the things that are required to get the business back on its feet," he says, adding, "the absence of options makes things easy. When there are many possible paths, choosing the best one is hard." The company downsized and sold off underperforming business units. "But, most important, during the time it took us to do the turnaround," McCallister says, "we kept asking what we wanted the company to look like after we'd cleaned it up."

Driving a Stake in the Ground

"Most of my team and I had been in the industry for decades, and we'd all seen the good, the bad, and the ugly in health insurance. With that history, we began by ruthlessly dissecting the state of the industry," he says. "Then we examined our history as well as our competitors', studied all the successes and failures, and evaluated what our competitors were doing and their financial performance, looking for a way to compete."

McCallister says, "We eventually had to agree with what customers of health insurance companies had been saying for years: that the health insurance value proposition was horrible. We decided that if your customers don't think much of the service you're giving them and you're not making any money doing it, then it must be irreparably broken.

"We decided to drive a stake in the ground," McCallister says, "and stop acting like our competitors and pretending that everything was okay." True to his belief that you must get things out in the open, he made a bold break with his health-benefit CEO peers. "We were going to say publicly that health insurance was broken and no longer defend it. In the U.S. economy," he says, "if a company delivers a bad product or service they get crushed, but health insurance providers still get paid when they're bad. It doesn't make any sense."

That bold new admission was followed by actions that would tackle this broken system. "Anyone can say that something is broken," he says. "The real question is, What are you going to do it fix it?" McCallister and his team began by asking the question, What can we learn from the rest of the economy that can be useful to us in health care? They came to several conclusions.

"Our first conclusion," he says with a grin, "was that the Internet was going to change everything." He grins because only a few years earlier, Humana had studied the impact of the Internet and decided it was just a toy with no business benefit. "Then we studied the overall economy and concluded that two thirds of it are driven by consumer spending, and that what drives consumer spending is transparency of price and quality." McCallister's team began wrestling with what their observations could mean to Humana and the health-care industry, and eventually landed on a few more conclusions that would guide their drive forward.

"The more we studied the industry the more obvious it became," says McCallister, "that the only people who could fix health-care were consumers. Everything else had been tried and found wanting, but we'd never turned to the power of consumers. Doctors and hospitals weren't going to fix health care and health insurance companies had proven themselves incapable of fixing it. Consumers have been responsible for transforming virtually all facets of our economic system," he says, reciting the oft-repeated mantra, "the customer is king, so why not help them change health care, too?" He started in his own backyard. "I encouraged our associates to embrace the change," responding to the health-care crisis by both listening to consumers and leading them. And he has made a point throughout his tenure of trying out the company's new, consumer-oriented benefits products with Humana's own employees first, re-fining and improving them before bringing the products to market.

But first he had to figure out how to get consumers the kind of actionable information they need in order to transform health care, enabling them to make the kind of empowered decisions typical of the rest of their purchasing lives.

"Most consumers know nothing about health care," he says. "They stumble around aimlessly within the system, they trust everybody, and they shouldn't and they've never had the tools to be powered up."

McCallister and his team quickly realized that health insurance companies possessed an invaluable asset—a comprehensive picture, through data, of the whole health-care experience from diagnosis to recovery, and everywhere in between. "Doctors only know what goes on in their offices. Laboratories only know the tests they administer and hospitals only know about the services they provide. But because we're the financial glue of the system," he says, "every transaction passes through us and we know about every doctor's visit, hospital admission, test taken, and medication prescribed.

"Follow the bouncing ball," McCallister says passionately, "health care was broken, the consumer had to fix it, they needed information to do so, and we had the information they needed. Ask yourself," he says, "what was missing?

"What was missing was the right structure of premiums and benefits to bring consumers into the game—to make them financially engaged with their health insurance," says McCallister. In other words, they needed to have some skin in the game. McCallister believes one of the reasons for soaring health-care premiums at other insurance companies is that consumers have been led to believe that doctor visits only cost the $10 copay and that prescriptions cost $5. "We had to unwind that mind-set and give them a financial stake in their health care."

After a rigorous analysis led them to choose "Guidance when you need it most" as Humana's promise to its clients, McCallister realized that this was the approach needed to transform Humana into a consumer company. "We thought a lot about adopting the guidance perspective," he recalls. "We want people to do much more than what they're doing now in this complicated system, and the only way they can do it is with the help and guidance of an entity with the actionable information they need to become true consumers of health care." Humana soon began to overhaul its health plans to make room for the growing phenomenon of consumerism.

The company decided that every customer would have his or her own easily understood, customizable dashboard, called SmartSummary, allowing each person to review plan benefits; view claims information; assess every doctor and dental visit; list every prescription; locate physicians, pharmacies, and dentists; compare hospitals' performance; use financial and budgeting tools; send and receive secured e-mails from Humana; learn ways to save money; create and maintain a personal health record; and search for pharmacy benefits and drug information. Humana also launched a sophisticated benefits-selection online "wizard," a multipayer claims portal for doctors and hospitals and partnered with a Milwaukee-based business coalition to create a national model for health-benefits transparency and cost containment.

McCallister decided that all of Humana's 26,000 employees would be required to manage their own health insurance electronically and sold the idea to them aggressively. He began by informing the work force that the company was no longer going to provide the same insurance policy to everyone; individuals and families would be able to choose the coverage they wanted or needed and would be in charge of their own insurance. Alternating between telling employees the company was on a mission to save trees and threatening to take a computer from desk to desk and teach noncomputer-savvy personnel how to push the keys, the company instituted online-only plan enrollments and relentlessly eliminated paper.

"Does everyone here love being in charge of their own health insurance and doing it electronically?" asks McCallister. "The answer is no. When we began the program eight years ago," he says, "about one third of our associates loved it, another third didn't care, and the final third hated it. I'd guess those numbers haven't changed very much but we have 100 percent of our people on high-deductible, low-premium health plans, virtually everything is done electronically, everyone makes contributions to their own spending accounts, use of money-saving generics is extraordinarily high, and we've got costs under control. There's nothing you'll ever do that everyone will love. If we're able to fully replicate what we've done inside the company with all our customers we'll have dramatically and irrevocably improved health care in America."

Humana's internal cost reductions have been nothing short of astounding. While annual health insurance cost increases have averaged in double digits for the past few years, Humana's cost of insuring its work force has only increased by an average of 4 percent per year since 2001, just slightly more than inflation. "We've saved tens of millions of dollars on our own health insurance costs," he says, "and the savings started as soon as we got people financially engaged. Since health care is such a huge piece of compensation, this has enabled us to do a lot more for our associates."

The Perils of Taking a Strong Position

Driving stakes into the ground allows a leader to provide a clear vision about what the company is, where it's headed, and how it's going to get there so it can hit the ground running. But it isn't for the faint hearted.

"In 2000, when I drove the stake in the ground and started talking about how health care was broken, and that the answer for fixing it didn't exist in Washington, D.C., but instead existed in the pocketbooks of customers," says McCallister, "everyone looked at me like I was dumber than a post.

"We chose to be at the leading edge. When you make that choice," he says, "people are going to call you names and throw dirt at you." Human nature says it's better for one's reputation to fail conventionally than to succeed unconventionally. But McCallister is undeterred. He has the fortitude to work through the "failure in the middle" phase of a long-term goal that causes many otherwise effective leaders to turn back.

He concludes, "The industry is a whole lot better off because of the stake we drove into the ground and the success we've enjoyed, because the conversation is different than it was. Now the other health insurance companies are talking about who has the better consumer-focused idea instead of just calling our idea dumb."

Once you've driven a stake in the ground you have to talk about it and promote it relentlessly. "We want to change the way the world does health care," says McCallister, "and we want to do it in the private sector. So we talk about it constantly with our employees, our customers, our competitors, legislators, and anyone else willing to listen."

Although McCallister admits that it can be exhausting advocating the same idea every day, he avoids monotony by conceiving new changes the industry can adopt. "I feel like the Pied Piper and in order to have people follow me and change the world, part of the job is playing the flute all the time. The problem with most businesses," he says, "is that instead of driving a stake in the ground, they stick a toe in the water and when it all gets hard or boring they start thinking about it too much, begin questioning their decision and pull their toe out, changing things, and starting all over again."

Hit the Ground Running Rule 6
Drive a Stake in the Ground

It's vitally important to let your workers, customers, and partners know who you are, what business you're in, and where you're headed. It creates clarity and that clarity defuses a lot of potentially toxic feelings as people have no question about what the boss thinks is "right" and important. His expectations are now predictable and nobody need worry about being second-guessed when making on-the-spot decisions.

But you can't drive a stake into the ground and forget about it. People need regular reinforcement. You have to constantly talk about and celebrate it as your reason for existence.

Mike McCallister's rules for transforming businesses into highly successful enterprises include:

- Don't be a jerk. There's no payoff in it.
- Figure out who controls your customers; get and stay close to them.
- Stop wringing your hands. Just do what needs to be done.
- Don't be intimidated by anyone.
- Be honest with everyone, especially those who can help you.
- Verify that people know what they're talking about.
- Resolve problems out in the open and quickly.
- Own the decisions you make. No waffling.
- Figure out what the right details are and pay attention to them.
- Let people know that something positive is happening.
- Drive a big stake into the ground.

Rule 7: Simplify Everything

My telephone rang shortly after 6:00 in the morning. "This is Jeff Lorberbaum from Mohawk Industries. I understand you want to talk to me. Why?"

The call was a breakthrough. For months we'd been trying to make arrangements to gain access to this CEO with no luck. When we finally met in Georgia, Lorberbaum began the meeting by saying, "Our focus has always been on running a successful business, not talking about how we accomplish that success," explaining that even his family's original plan to take the company public "scared us to death because we were afraid our operating secrets might be revealed.

"When my father started Aladdin Mills (Mohawk's predecessor), he focused relentlessly on speed, simplicity, and efficiency, and that's my focus at Mohawk Industries today."

Aladdin Mills

Jeff's father, Alan Lorberbaum, fought as an infantryman in World War II. When he returned he earned a degree in textile engineering from Lowell Textile Institute and then was summoned to Dalton,

Georgia, where his family ran a business manufacturing bedspreads and other chenille products.

Dalton, Georgia, had become a hotbed of textile manufacturing because of women in the area who'd revived "candlewicking," a pre-Civil War method of creating tufted bedspreads by inserting loops of yarn into a patterned backing. Droves of people converged on Dalton to purchase bedspreads, and it wasn't long before an enterprising engineer copied their process and built a machine (using a single-needle Singer sewing machine) that manufactured carpet the same way, by tufting yarn onto a jute backing.

Until the late 1950s, carpet—woven exclusively from wool—was an expensive luxury few families could afford. In fact, it was so costly that between 1899 and 1965 per-household shipments of carpet never changed and averaged only four square yards per home annually. But restrictions on the use of wool during World War II hastened research into synthetic fibers such as nylon and acrylic. Alan Lorberbaum and other industry pioneers realized these new man-made fibers would change the industry.

In 1957, Lorberbaum left his family business and with savings of $10,000 struck out on his own. He founded Aladdin Mills in a former roller skating rink, manufacturing rugs out of the leftover waste products generated by the polypropylene (plastics) industry, which became the basis for the company's future expansion into the carpet industry.

"When my father got into the business there were very few barriers to entry," says current Mohawk CEO Jeff Lorberbaum. "Anyone could get into the business without any money," adding that raw materials used to produce yarn came from large chemical companies and that converters to turn the raw material into useable product were widely available. "You could call yourself a carpet manufacturer," he says, "and not have any real assets." Only a few years after Alan Lorberbaum founded Aladdin Mills, more than four hundred carpet manufacturers dotted the countryside around Dalton, Georgia. By then the city had become the carpet capital of the world. Lorberbaum knew Aladdin Mills had to be managed differently or would risk getting lost in the melee.

Lorberbaum started by manufacturing small, synthetic bath mats that regional carpet distributors sold to fast-growing retail discount chains that in turn sold the rugs to consumers for only a few dollars apiece. "No legitimate carpet manufacturer would have done what my father did," says Lorberbaum. "The industry had very small margins (averaging only 2 or 3 percent) and my father's decision to specialize in a very narrow product line eventually necessitated certain manufacturing practices: Wring out waste, create efficiencies of scale, and achieve a high volume."

One of the most important lessons I've learned from researching the stories of the world's fastest growing, most productive, and successful companies is that tight margins are often our best friends in business because they force us to find solutions we would otherwise never consider. Many successful businesses were built by entrepreneurs who were forced to improvise, adapt, and overcome big challenges like impossibly tight margins. Aladdin Mills is another case in point. Later you'll see how the big challenges it faced successfully manufacturing bath mats for discounters created the foundation for its phenomenal focus on simplicity, adaptability, and making strategy by doing.

Jeff Lorberbaum says Aladdin Mills was truly a family business. "There was no difference between personal life and business life in my family. My mother worked alongside my father, and all of the kids worked in the factory as laborers for minimum wage during summers." He says that his father was a taskmaster like many of his generation. "He probably fired me once a week." But his dad also taught him what it really takes to be a great entrepreneur. "My father worked twelve hours a day, seven days a week, and always told people that he got more joy out of business than he would have from conducting the New York Philharmonic Orchestra."

By the time Jeff Lorberbaum was ready to go to college the business was going strong and growing. "The company was the family, and the family was the company. Every cent went back into the company to make it bigger, better, and faster. Our only goal," he says, "was to achieve as much growth as we could."

Jeff Lorberbaum

Lorberbaum left Georgia to attend the University of Denver in Colorado, where he earned a degree in finance. "I picked that school because of those that accepted me, it was the farthest away from home. Like a lot of young people, I needed to get away for while and see more of the world.

"I started out as a math major," he says, "and kept changing majors trying to figure out what I wanted to do." Along the way Lorberbaum gained a broad mathematical background and experience with early computers (this was the seventies). After graduation, he hadn't yet decided on a career path, so he headed home and went to work at Aladdin. "I think," he says self-effacingly, "that it was probably the only job I could get."

Lorberbaum estimates that when he returned to the company in the mid 1970s the business was doing about $40 million in annual revenues, but there were still no titles, no organizational charts, or computers. His father still ran the company from the top down and made every decision. Lorberbaum initially was assigned a job in scheduling and eventually worked every job in the company. His father told him his job title was OIT, *Owner in Training*.

Seeking Competitive Advantages

Until the early 1980s chemical companies had cornered the process of fiber extrusion* but in the Lorberbaums' constant search for ways to simplify the business and contain raw material costs, Aladdin Mills became one of the first carpet mills to backward integrate manufacturing by purchasing an extrusion unit to produce its own fiber. "It took us two years to get the machinery working," says Lorberbaum, "but once we did it gave us a significant competitive advantage."

Surveying the competitive landscape, the Lorberbaum family noted that another carpet company was beginning to consolidate the industry. The Lorberbaums redoubled their efforts to make their business more efficient, take charge of their own destiny, and differentiate themselves in the marketplace rather than risk becoming irrelevant.

"By the early 1980s we'd expanded beyond bath mats and room-sized rugs to manufacturing rolls of broadloom carpet, but we were still producing commodity products, which most everyone in the industry avoided because these products had the lowest margins. Just as we invested in extrusion to improve Aladdin's manufacturing efficiencies," says Lorberbaum, "we forward integrated our processes by building a national distribution system. This provided us with differentiated service and helped to build direct relationships with retailers, a key to future success as the era of regional distributors acting as intermediaries between manufacturers and retailers was coming to an end."

This common sense decision by Lorberbaum was very smart.

---

*Most synthetic and manufactured fibers are created by "extrusion"—forcing a thick, viscous liquid the consistency of cold honey through the tiny holes of a device called a spinneret to form continuous filaments of semisolid polymer, which can be woven into carpet.

Earlier I shared a simple strategy for success at retail (have the right product, in the right place, for the right price, at the right time), but it's really hard to know the right product until the customer tells you what they want. In the eighties most carpet retailers had to guess and risk buying too much product that people didn't want or try to talk their customers into waiting weeks for a special order. By making Aladdin's product line available the "next day," the company made it simpler for their customers (the retailers) to satisfy even the pickiest consumer. And when you make it simple for your customers to succeed you're going to get more of their business.

The company sent Mark Lorberbaum, Jeff's brother, to Miami to set up its first distribution center in Miami. "Any carpet store in south Florida could place an order and have it delivered the next day," Jeff says. "We targeted the smallest retailers who were willing to pay a premium for that level of service.

"We didn't have national distribution of Aladdin products, and there were huge holes on the map where we didn't have any business. It was a delicate balancing act," Lorberbaum says, "because we didn't want to alienate our present customers that were providing the distribution of our products. To protect the business relationships we had, we decided to expand the distribution center concept by setting them up in areas where our products weren't sold at the time."

Aladdin staffed its distribution centers with entrepreneurs and set them free to run the business as though it was their own and build strong relationships with the retailers. "The complete autonomy we gave the managers of our distribution centers became our next big competitive advantage," says Lorberbaum, "because when these guys walked into a retail store they didn't have any rules they had to follow. They'd identify customers, find out what they needed, and sell it below cost if that's what it took to get other profitable business. It became impossible to compete with our distribution centers because there wasn't a strategy anyone could copy; they created a unique strategy for every customer."

Efforts by Alan and Jeff Lorberbaum to keep filling holes in the map and create their own national distribution network proved highly successful. Throughout the 1980s and 1990s the company enjoyed robust growth of 20 percent annually, but the success didn't create a false sense of security for the Lorberbaum family.

"We were generating hundreds of millions of dollars in annual revenue with only five or six senior managers by keeping the business exceedingly simple," says Lorberbaum. "We offered a narrow line of high-volume commodity products and differentiated these with our delivery system and an emphasis on exceptional customer service. On paper we were highly successful but every cent of our profits was reinvested in the bricks and mortar and equipment of the company.

"Every year new equipment was being developed that produced carpet significantly faster than the year before," says Lorberbaum, "and we had to buy it and remain the most efficient or otherwise, we'd have lost our competitive edge. There was no way we could outgrow our capital needs, and for every dollar we earned, we were borrowing two and putting it all back into the business." By the early 1990s Aladdin's annual revenues topped $450 million, and the company was among the top five carpet manufacturers in the nation but because of the huge capital needs associated with the business, money was always tight.

Lorberbaum says, "As fast as we were expanding through internal growth, both Mohawk and Shaw were driving the industry toward consolidation through acquisitions, and they were growing even faster than we were. To compete long term, we had to expand faster than ever before. My father and I looked at Mohawk, which had grown to $800 million in annual revenues, and Shaw, which had grown to around the same size or bigger and we decided that we had to do things on a larger scale. That," he says, "was going to require money that we didn't have."

The Lorberbaum family, the first carpet supplier to Home Depot when that company began selling carpet in its stores, drove to Atlanta and met with Bernie Marcus, one of the founders of the company, explained their dilemma, told him they were thinking about going public to raise cash, and asked his advice. Marcus directed them to an investment banker who'd been one of the cofounders of Home Depot. "After talking with a number of investment banks we finally decided we'd go public and sell 25 percent of the company," says Lorberbaum, adding, "we were very nervous because we'd never told anybody anything about our business, treated everything as a secret, and kept our business very confidential. We were not excited about the prospect of doing road shows to attract potential investors."

Two weeks before the planned public offering was scheduled, a banker representing Mohawk Industries expressed interest in buying Aladdin Mills. The prospect of avoiding a public offering and immediately obtaining a highly competitive market position was a great relief to the Lorberbaum family and they decided to listen.

Mohawk offered the family $400 million in stock in exchange for their company, Aladdin Mills. "We didn't even know if it was a good offer but saw many exceptional opportunities with the Mohawk offer," says Lorberbaum. "We were scared of going public, we didn't understand it or know what the heck it was, so we accepted their offer because we wanted to focus on quickly establishing a leading position in a rapidly consolidating industry."

One might imagine that the family had cause for great celebration after living conservatively for many years, but that wasn't the case. "On the evening the sale became complete my parents and I drove around our factories and talked about all of the years of hard work and sacrifice that had been required to reach that point. We didn't have a sense of satisfaction. My parents felt as though they'd sold one of their children," says Lorberbaum. "The business had been their life and suddenly somebody else owned it."

Not interested in the limelight, Alan Lorberbaum had named

Jeff as president of Aladdin a year before the company was sold in anticipation of going public. The purchase agreement with Mohawk contractually kept the management of Aladdin intact and ensured only limited changes could be made without the approval of the family.

"Everyone kept telling us that we owned Mohawk because with 45 percent of their stock we were the largest shareholder. What they said fell on deaf ears," he says, "because we were all afraid Mohawk would screw it up and that we'd all be gone. We were afraid of Mohawk and afraid of the papers we signed."

One year after the sale, Jeff Lorberbaum was still the president of Aladdin, but his father withdrew from the business he'd built, the family's stock in Mohawk had fallen in value by two thirds, Mohawk was having difficulty integrating all the companies it had purchased, the price of raw materials was skyrocketing, and Mohawk was still recovering from the collapse of several factory roofs during the worst snowstorm in history. Lorberbaum had seen the potential opportunities represented by becoming a part of Mohawk Industries. Given the circumstances that arose following the acquisition, his leadership mettle would be tested as never before.

Mohawk Industries

Mohawk Industries, the company that purchased the Lorberbaum family business, got its start as Mohawk Carpet Mills in 1878 when four brothers imported fourteen used carpet looms from England and set up a factory in Amsterdam, New York.

Mohawk was managed by members of the founding Shuttleworth family until 1980. The company, then called Mohasco, had completed a series of acquisitions that had taken the company's focus away from its core carpet business and created some financial challenges. The company recruited an outsider, David Kolb, to take the reins of Mohasco Carpet as president. Kolb, a highly regarded

140

leader in the industry, took the carpet company private in a leveraged buyout, got the company profitable again, and then took the carpet manufacturing business public again as Mohawk Industries. With the money raised, he embarked on a nonstop whirlwind series of acquisitions that lasted more than fifteen years. Kolb says the most important and the best acquisition he ever made was the Lorberbaum family's Aladdin Mills.

"I had three rules for acquisitions," he says. "First, we needed to know we'd be able to integrate the company, we wouldn't overpay, and the final rule was that we wouldn't lose sales by cannibalizing another area of the company."

Aladdin was the largest company Kolb acquired during his career and says it was a perfect fit. "They were almost the same size as Mohawk, so we effectively doubled the size of the company," he says. "They'd focused on polypropylene while we'd concentrated on nylon, they had their own trucking and warehouse facilities that would assist our distribution, and their products sold at a lower price point than ours. Alan Lorberbaum was truly a manufacturing genius, and Jeff did such a great job operating Aladdin that after a year we named him chief operating officer of Mohawk."

"The division I ran was doing well," says Lorberbaum, "but Mohawk needed to have an integrated business strategy across all of its divisions. Besides," he jokes, "no one else wanted the job."

The marriage between Kolb and Lorberbaum turned out to be a match made in heaven, and every skill about simplifying business practice that Lorberbaum's father had spent a lifetime teaching Jeff was about to pay off. "Dave Kolb's vision for consolidating the industry was extraordinary," Lorberbaum says. "He kept driving growth and whenever an opportunity to buy a company arose he jumped at it. When I became COO the business was operating in pieces and parts with a broken infrastructure and not maximizing its potential. Other than that everything was *perfect*."

Mohawk Industries was a collection of carpet companies making similar products, eventually sold to similar clients, on similar equipment. A real risk (and one that confronts many companies) was that the company would be cannibalized by customers playing one operating division against another in search of better pricing and that salespeople, paid on commission, wouldn't care less if they were stealing business from another division of the same company.

Lorberbaum began his integration efforts by redefining the company's sales, product, manufacturing, and marketing strategies, and Kolb (perhaps influenced by the Lorberbaum family's commanding ownership stake in the company) agreed to postpone further acquisitions until the infrastructure was in place. "The time had come," Lorberbaum says, "to say 'time out' and stop buying companies until we had everything structured and running smoothly. Otherwise, you find yourself so overwhelmed and unable to execute that you don't know where in the heck to start?"

In redefining Mohawk Industries and preparing the organization to quickly become the largest floor-covering company in the world, Lorberbaum used the following tactics, many learned from his father.

Make Everything as Simple as Possible

Jeff Lorberbaum is not a fan of most business books. "I have about fifty management and leadership books on the shelf. When I go on vacations I start reading them but finish very few. Most of them have little value. Some of the authors assign complicated titles to simple ideas and treat it as a new concept. Much of the academic stuff doesn't have any practical application."

Mohawk's deep-thinking CEO makes a good point. Everything should be made as simple as possible, not the other way around.

At Mohawk, making everything simple starts with speaking plainly and without using high-sounding buzzwords or complicated MBA jargon. When asked why Mohawk entered the carpet-padding business, Lorberbaum replies, "We needed to fill up the darn trucks and cover part of the overhead." Likewise, Lorberbaum outlined his marketing strategy in words anyone could understand. "In our business, the consumer doesn't just come in and say 'I like this. Give it to me.' There's a salesperson in between who controls the choices. These salespeople don't want any problems, so they tend to promote the products that they have the least problems with and most confidence in. We changed our service model so that the retailer gets what the consumer wants a day or two after the order is placed. Sometimes our service level is higher than the customer's requirement, but that's a reason salespeople prefer Mohawk."

Really brilliant people force themselves to say important things simply. Albert Einstein himself lived by the maxim, "If a scientific theory cannot be explained so that a child can understand, it's probably worthless." Simplifying starts with the effort to speak plainly.

Making things simple also means untangling challenges from a lot of personal issues and extra baggage so you can see new ways to solve nagging problems. "Most people get confused with the complexities," Lorberbaum observes. "They are encumbered by stuff that won't let them move forward. What I try to do is start with a blank sheet of paper, write down what I'd like the process to look like, and create the 'perfect' solution. Then if you can't achieve the perfect solution, you ask, 'How close can I get?' Maybe it's not 100 percent, but you can get 70 percent and that's a dramatic improvement. Oversimplify it. It forces you to think things through and lets you be more adaptive."

Do It Incrementally

"Most companies decide to jump from point A to point Z as quickly as possible—they decide on the end game and throw all the chips on the table," says Lorberbaum. "I've never been willing to do that.

"The problem with gigantic leaps," he explains, "is that people fail to take into consideration all the unforeseen obstacles that will happen along the way. I've yet to find a situation where I started at one point and anticipated all of the circumstances that would arise.

"We try to define a long-term strategy but focus on an incremental step that we can execute, implement that step, and then reevaluate the end game again," he says. "Usually you're not too far off your objective and then adjust your next step to exceed your original expectation."

Conventional wisdom says that business is like chess, where the winner will be the one who's thinking ten moves ahead. Undoubtedly this image motivates many leaders to make plans way beyond their ability to accurately anticipate. But Lorberbaum understands that it's often better to be right about your next move rather than strategizing over the next ten moves. As a local New York chess player explained to the stunned crowd wondering how he beat the mighty Capablanca (one of the world's most renown chess strategists), "I may only think one move ahead—but it is always the best move."

Lorberbaum is sold on the advantages of simplicity and short-term decision loops where you observe, decide, act, and get feedback over and over. "When you take smaller steps, you're able to pause, test your assumptions, reevaluate your big objective, and adjust the steps as required. Companies make huge financial commitments to massive change," he says, "and then discover they can't execute because their assumptions are now so different from reality." Lorberbaum also argues that many companies become so self-centered and focused on their own change efforts that their customers get completely forgotten in the process, leaving the company more vulnerable than it was in the beginning.

Lorberbaum decided that his first goal as COO was to get Mohawk operating as efficiently and simply as Aladdin. He started by fixing and integrating manufacturing because he knew that process and was most comfortable with it. "All the plants were aligned by brand," he says, "and our first change was to have them manufactured by product type. Mohawk had been driven by marketing and Aladdin by simplicity, so we promoted a talented group of Aladdin managers and sent them to restructure Mohawk's methodologies and systems. At times," he says, "it was like trying to merge Ferrari and Volkswagen factories, but we took it one step at a time and stopped reacting to our competitors, simplified the raw material components, shut down and consolidated plants, and fixed the information systems."

Following manufacturing, Lorberbaum tackled information systems, marketing and branding, sales, and distribution. He says his greatest regret is that he didn't throw out all the information systems on day one and start fresh. "We were operating with homegrown systems that couldn't talk to each other and manage the complexity of the operation," he says, "and it was a constant impediment to simplifying everything."

In two years time, Lorberbaum says they had everything reasonably integrated and under control and the company was profitably expanding.

Capitalize on Good Fortune

Many CEOs are quick to claim the credit for everything good that happens (even if they had nothing to do with it) and equally quick to distance themselves from and point fingers of blame when something bad happens. Not so with Lorberbaum, who is fast to accept responsibility when something doesn't work out and eager to admit when Lady Luck smiles on him and the company he leads.

At the same time Lorberbaum was taking operational control at Mohawk, the company's largest rival, Shaw Industries, made a business decision that provided Mohawk some breathing room—time to get its act together and hit the ground running again. "Sometimes you fall into things," says Lorberbaum, "and that's what happened when we were trying to integrate and simplify everything. Capitalizing on that good fortune is a key component of success.

"Shaw has always been a good competitor," says Lorberbaum, "but their decision to enter the retail market did not go as they planned." Recognizing that carpet manufacturers essentially provide free financing for carpet stores, Shaw decided to get into retail and started buying carpet stores and chains all across the country. "They purchased a significant share of retail flooring sales, but the volumes those stores generated were small compared to their manufacturing revenues," Lorberbaum says. "I don't know exactly how much revenue they were generating in their own stores, but for example's sake, assume they were doing $500 million annually in their stores. The problem is they were putting the other two or three billion they were doing with independent retailers at risk."

Shaw couldn't aggressively operate its own retail stores because it was competing against its own customers. Lorberbaum says, "Shaw created a plan and implemented it, but failed to recognize the impact the plan had on existing customers. Their conflicting strategies gave Mohawk's leadership team an opportunity to realign our business and improve our execution."

Don't Force Things

What do you do when you're up to your ears with integration challenges and yet new opportunities just keep knocking? Jeff Lorberbaum's simple common sense gave him the answer.

Lorberbaum was incredibly busy integrating the scores of acquired companies that were now part of the Mohawk portfolio. CEO David Kolb was still on the lookout for attractive acquisitions and found some sweet opportunities. The two came to an unusual accommodation. Each time an opportunity arose to buy another company that was too good to pass up, they agreed to buy it but postpone making any operational changes.

"When an opportunity to buy a business comes along, you either take advantage of it or pass on the opportunity," Lorberbaum says. "Dave Kolb and I believed that Mohawk had to be positioned properly to take advantage of opportunities, particularly when your own business is evolving and the market is driving changes in the business." So Lorberbaum understood that *not* buying when the opportunity presented itself wouldn't be a good decision.

On the other hand, Lorberbaum's common sense told him that giving in to the urge to do something when you haven't had time to think, especially when you are making a move that you've never made before, is not a good decision. "In the South we use a lot of colorful expressions," Lorberbaum explains, "Like 'You never bet the farm.' In other words, keep the risks at a level where you can recover if things don't pan out.

"It was up to me to integrate the various acquisitions," Lorberbaum concludes. "We would acquire a company knowing that we would make no major changes to its infrastructure until we had completed existing plans to satisfy Mohawk's existing needs.

"One year we bought five companies," he says, "and it would have been impossible to immediately force our culture of efficiency and simplicity onto their organizations. So we let their existing management teams continue to run the companies and accepted their operational results until we were capable of integrating them."

Ultimately the acquisitions were successful. Surprisingly, according to Lorberbaum, the right answers came "from a lot of dedicated people who overpowered the maze of challenges with their own internal strengths and instincts and made it work. Throughout Mohawk's growth, I have always been fortunate to have a strong, capable team, and one of Mohawk's strengths as a company is the leadership that we've assembled from all of those different acquisitions."

Use Silos

Everyone agrees that operational silos inevitably lead to turf building and battles and a lack of communication that can threaten the health of the organization. It's been such a hot topic (verging on becoming another business buzzword) that Amazon.com lists 166 books about breaking down silos while a Google search turns up more than 2 million hits listing articles, books, papers, and discussions on the subject. Jeff Lorberbaum disagrees.

"We were business-unit driven," says Lorberbaum, "with each unit doing their own thing with disregard for the good of the whole company. I selected talented people who could manage important functions (marketing, sales, advertising, etc.)," he says. "I directed them to create holistic functions that serve the entire company.

"Each person who headed a function," says Lorberbaum, "determined how to realign disparate assets, operating independently, and create a cohesive entity, without regard for culture, history, brands, and products. By taking a functionally driven approach," Lorberbaum says, "we were able to gain tremendous focus, eliminate waste and gain simplicity. I don't think we could have done all the things we accomplished without the silos, but, like with every good story, there was also bad news.

"The functional silos we created served a valuable purpose that allowed us to hit the ground running and gain velocity," he says. "Eventually, over a period of a few years, they began operating too independently. That was detrimental to the entire organization and it was time to collapse them again." Showing his adaptability, when it became time to collapse the silos, Lorberbaum changed them back into business units but not into anything resembling what they looked like originally.

As much as we want the certainty of "one right answer" and as much as gurus would like us to believe there truly is one right answer, it's simply not the case. Silos work and they don't work; centralization works and doesn't work; even command and control can be the right tactic at times. Lorberbaum has learned that the one right answer depends on the circumstances. And then, when those circumstances change, you have to be adaptable enough to let go. "Keep an open mind" is his advice to new leaders.

Leverage Assets

In 2001, when Dave Kolb turned sixty, he retired and Jeff Lorberbaum became CEO. "It was uneventful and seamless," says Lorberbaum, "because we were always on the same page and worked so well together. In fact, hardly a day goes by that I don't use him as a sounding board.

"You can approach a business two ways," says Lorberbaum, "either be a growth business or figure out how to maximize the cash out of your existing business. We have always been committed to being a growth business."

While serving as the company's COO prior to becoming CEO, Lorberbaum looked at the carpet business and realized the market couldn't indefinitely sustain the desired growth. Companies sustained high double-digit growth through the mid 1990s as industrywide sales catapulted to over a billion square yards of carpet annually. But, as the decade evolved, consumers were beginning replace some of their wall-to-wall carpeting with hard surfaces like ceramic tiles, wood, and stone.

"Our growth strategy was to broaden the product base and the incremental step was to become a distributor of hard-surface products. In the late 1990s, we initiated a limited test with ceramic tile in the Florida market. That pilot program reassured us that we could leverage our broad customer base and delivery systems to successfully enter other flooring markets. Going into the 2001 recession, we added warehouses to stock the material, started sourcing products as a distributor, and hired 250 salespeople to bring the hard-surface line to market. Like before," says Lorberbaum, "we made every darn mistake you could make; our system limitations impeded progress, consumer product preference varied by geographical region, each product had unique needs, and our people had to learn the market."

Despite all the speed bumps encountered, Lorberbaum's SOP of one incremental step at a time paid off again, and the company began adding $100 million in revenue each year in hard-surface sales. "Even though we faced many unexpected challenges," he says, "the big win was the realization that we could leverage the carpet business with the hard-surface business, gain more commitment from our customers, and improve both businesses simultaneously."

Speed Up Trends

Most companies try to slow down developing trends for several reasons. The infrastructure of most companies isn't conducive to moving rapidly; they want to make sure they're fully ready to capitalize on new trends before their competitors, but more practically they want to milk the old cow as long as they're able. By contrast, Lorberbaum and Mohawk have been the drivers of almost every innovation in floor coverings. "Even though we were a carpet company," says Lorberbaum, "I really believe we helped speed up the transition of the retail market to total flooring suppliers because of the legitimacy we brought to the use of hard surfaces. By educating our retail customers about our expanded product offerings, we helped them to create more complete flooring showrooms instead of carpet stores."

Let the Best Idea Win

In 2002, Mohawk Industries acquired Dal-Tile, one of the world's largest manufacturers, distributors, and retailers of ceramic tile for $1.7 billion in a friendly acquisition. It turns out that Dal-Tile, led by Goodyear veteran and turnaround specialist Jacques Sardas, had been conducting an in-house study about where they wanted to take the company. They had concluded that their vision of the future looked a lot like Mohawk's. "It was a straightforward transaction," says Lorberbaum. "They decided to sell, and they didn't want an auction. We liked what we saw, they liked us, and we completed the deal."

The acquisition of Dal-Tile signaled another change in strategy for Lorberbaum and Mohawk Industries. "We'd completed more than fourteen acquisitions since the company went public," he says, "and had worked zealously to integrate all of them, drive out costs, waste, and inefficiency, and simplify them. With Dal-Tile, we decided to leave them as a standalone entity because ceramic tile had unique market drivers."

When asked if Dal-Tile has learned lessons about simplification and driving out inefficiency from Mohawk, Lorberbaum makes a surprising admission that very few CEO's egos would allow. "We learned a lot more from them than they did from us. Mohawk," he says, "was led by people who grew up in small businesses and were so close to the business that they were touching it every day and instinctively knew what to do. While we were still running Mohawk like a small business," says Lorberbaum, "Dal-Tile had in place goals, objectives, and metrics for everyone from the factory floor to the secretaries and the executives. We embraced those things, integrated them into Mohawk, and became an infinitely better company as a result. The most significant concept we asked them to embrace was our value of total commitment to customer service from quality to delivery."

Lorberbaum further displayed his willingness to embrace the best idea even if it was somebody else's by opening up the corporate checkbook. "When Jacques Sardas took over at Dal-Tile," he says, "the company was technically bankrupt, and they'd spent five years paring down debt levels, generating cash, and spending very little money. When we bought them, we asked, 'How much do you need to grow because we want to grow the heck out of this company.' We changed our strategy of focusing only on eliminating waste and inefficiency and were ready to invest for growth and started investing in new facilities, new product lines, increased distribution, and more sales personnel."

The other lesson Lorberbaum learned from Dal-Tile was the value of moving people around, and he's embraced it as heartily as Ron Sargent, CEO of Staples. "One disadvantage of having grown the company as a collection of small businesses," Lorberbaum says, "was the tendency that when someone had learned a job well, we had them stay in the same job, doing the same thing and living in the same town for their entire career. I've learned," he says, "that it's far better to move talented people around, keep adding to their responsibilities, challenging them, and letting the cream rise to the top. We're not where we want to be, but it's a dramatic change from the way we operated before."

Don't Be Afraid to Change

Jeff Lorberbaum hit the ground running as a child when he went to work in his father's first factory and has never stopped. He credits his father with teaching him how to change things.

"The thing that limits most people and the reason they can't hit the ground running," he says, "is they get a predetermined goal in their head and can't let go; it stays there forever. What that means to organizations is that once they agree on something, they're always afraid to change it.

"If you're trying to climb one mountain and find that you can't reach the summit, you don't abandon mountain climbing," Lorberbaum says. "You change the goal and go for another summit. Who cares which mountain you climb? The view is great from every mountain top."

Today, with nearly $8 billion in annual sales, Mohawk Industries long ago passed its biggest rival (Warren Buffett's Shaw Industries) to become the largest floor-covering company in the world and the Lorberbaums' original $10,000 investment in Aladdin Mills is reputedly worth close to a billion dollars.

When asked how long he'll remain chairman and CEO of Mohawk Industries, Jeff Lorberbaum only says, "Old people look backwards and young people look forward. As long I'm looking forward, I'll be here. I inherited one other trait from my father: I love business, it's my hobby, what else would I do?"

Hit the Ground Running Rule 7
Simplify Everything

The timeless rules Jeff Lorberbaum (and his father before him) used to create the largest floor-covering company in the world include:

- Figure out what you can do to make your customers' lives easier.
- Ruthlessly wring out waste, complexity, and inefficiencies.
- Recognize and take advantage of good fortune.
- Figure out where you want to go but take the journey in small steps, pausing frequently to reassess.
- Leverage your assets to cover your costs and expand what you sell.
- Don't try to stop things from happening; speed up trends.
- Let the best idea win.
- Make everything as simple as possible.

Rule 8: Be Accountable

Marshall Larsen, chairman, president, and CEO of Goodrich, says that memories of his first days as a cadet at the U.S. Military Academy at West Point are just a blur.

"You show up with nothing," says Larsen. "You don't bring a suitcase, not even a toothbrush. You're issued a T-shirt, socks, and gym shorts with a name tag attached, get your head shaved, and spend the day learning how to salute and march. At the end of the day," he says, "you're given your first uniform and march with your company to Trophy Point on the Hudson River and are sworn in. That was followed by intense Cadet Basic Training and the beginnings of the traditional harassment of freshmen (plebes) by upperclassmen originally designed to help weed out those cadets who haven't got what it takes to make it.

"It's better now," he says, "but, when I was there, it wasn't uncommon for an upperclassman to sit outside a dormitory with another upperclassman waiting five stories up, call a plebe over, hand him a playing card, and tell him to run it upstairs to his buddy and be back within sixty seconds. When the freshman returned huffing and puffing," says Larsen, "the upperclassman would give him another card and tell him to do the same thing again and then continue though all fifty-two cards in the deck."

Larsen remembers that the academic program at West Point was perhaps the toughest in the nation. "It was advanced calculus six days a week for two years," he says, "and the rule was simple. If you failed one class you were out." Of the nearly 1,100 cadets who were appointed alongside Larsen, people began dropping within one week and by the time four years passed almost 350 were gone.

"It's a classic military tool," says Larsen, "to break people down, convince them they can't do it alone, and then put them back together as a unit." Larsen wasn't about to return home a failure and quickly learned that the only way to survive the tough conditions and demanding curriculum at West Point was by living the words, *"cooperate and graduate,"* that he frequently heard upperclassmen repeat.

The lessons learned at West Point and as an Army artillery captain served Larsen well during his climb from entry-level financial analyst to head of the world's leading aerospace and defense companies. His military background also provided him a better understanding of "accountability" that prepared him to hit the ground running when he landed the CEO's job.

Goodrich Corporation

BF Goodrich was founded by Dr. Benjamin Franklin Goodrich almost 140 years ago in Akron, Ohio, as a rubber company. Goodrich's storied past as a world-class innovations company includes having invented both vinyl and synthetic rubber, supplying the tires for Charles Lindbergh's transatlantic flight, inventing tubeless tires, creating the spacesuits for America's first astronauts, and even coining the word "zipper" in 1923.

You can still buy BF Goodrich tires, but they aren't made by the company that practically invented them (they're currently made by Michelin North America) and the company's name no longer starts with the initials of its founder. BF Goodrich exited the tire business more than twenty years ago and, at the turn of this century, dropped the initials to better reflect its status as a diversified aerospace and defense company with 24,000 employees in 90 factories around the world.

Goodrich is involved in three primary markets:

Commercial aerospace original equipment manufacturing (OEM)— The company designs and builds equipment found on almost every aircraft in the world, including landing gear on the Airbus A380, braking systems on Boeing's 787 Dreamliner, and hundreds of other components ranging from seating systems to cockpit lighting and ice detection systems.

Replacement parts—As aircraft components and systems wear out or require replacement, the company provides hundreds of replacement parts and systems as well as maintenance, repair, and overhaul services.

Defense and space—The company designs and builds systems including ejection seats, landing systems, laser awareness devices, and systems for weapon bays for military aircraft in both OEM and the aftermarket.

Marshall Larsen

Marshall Larsen's tiny hometown of Enderlin, North Dakota (population 901), was given its name by German settlers who called it "End-der-lin" because it was the railroad's last stop and, to their mind, it was the *end-of-the-line*. But Larsen, who got a big break in Enderlin, remembers it fondly as a great place to get started.

Larsen's father was a rural mail carrier with a refrigeration and air conditioning business on the side, and his mother was a stay-at-home mom until the kids hit high school when she went to work in a retail store to make additional money for the family.

"I had a great time growing up," says Larsen. "It was a little town, no one locked their doors, and there wasn't any crime." Larsen, who excelled at both academics and sports, went to the same school for twelve years in a building that had the grade school on the first floor and the high school upstairs. Larsen's part-time job was working in a local hardware store for an owner who gave him time off for high school sports and who hoped Larsen would get an education and return to Enderlin and buy his store.

That local store was also the site of Larsen's first big break. "One day a woman came into the store," he says, "and it turns out that she was the county chairwoman of the Democratic party. She asked if I'd ever thought about going to West Point. I told her I hadn't but she put the wheels in motion for me," he says. "The paperwork got filled out; she arranged for me to compete for an appointment by one of the state's U.S. senators. The next thing I knew I was taking my first airplane ride from Fargo, North Dakota, to New York City and up the Hudson River to West Point.

"The Vietnam War was going on at the time and, in the mid-sixties," he says, "young people weren't as adamantly opposed to it as they eventually became. If I'd gone to college I could have gotten a student exemption but would have faced being drafted later on. The more I thought about it," he says, "the more I realized I could kill two birds with one stone and get a great education and become an army officer."

The harassment of undergraduates by upperclassmen at West Point and other military academies is renowned, and Larsen says there are a "thousand ways" it happens. One of the tactics employed when Larsen was there was to call for a clothing formation with everyone dressed in fatigues. "As soon as we'd assemble," he says, "we were told we had two minutes to get back to our rooms, change into full dress uniform, and be back in formation. It was almost impossible to do," he says, "but we moved like there was no tomorrow because the first person back in line at attention got dismissed and the laggards kept getting harassed."

Room inspections were held immediately following the clothing drill and, if in haste, a cadet had failed to perfectly fold and hang the clothing he had changed from, he was issued demerits. "Enough demerits," says Larsen, "and you were out of West Point. To this day when I go golfing with my friends they're amazed that I'm showered and out of the locker room before they're out of their golf clothes."

Larsen doesn't have fond memories of his first year at West Point and promised that when it came his turn he wasn't going to take part in harassing underclassmen. "There were only a couple of times that I got on somebody for screwing up," he says, "but I didn't have time for the harassment thing because it never made any sense to me. When you enter the army as an officer you can't harass a private and you can't do it in business, so I never understood why it was tolerated there. A lot of the horrible harassment was done by students who'd been terribly mistreated themselves."

Larsen also learned a valuable lesson in tenacity from the harassment. "I decided I wasn't going to allow the upperclassmen who were harassing the hell out of people to get in the way of my objective, which was to get a great education and graduate as an officer." Later Larsen made zero tolerance for any form of harassment one of the centerpieces of the Goodrich culture.

Larsen is quick to add that besides the great education he gained at West Point, he also learned valuable life skills that have served him well. "I learned ethics, the honor system," he says, "accountability, and teamwork."

Following his graduation from West Point, with a degree in engineering, Larsen owed the U.S. Army five years of active service in return for his college education. He began by volunteering for the Army Airborne School where he leaned to parachute as a means of combat deployment. Next he attended the U.S. Army's advanced jump school followed by the famous Army Ranger School for an intensive course of study in combat leadership. Following the completion of officer basic training school, Larsen was assigned to Fort Carson, Colorado.

"If you ever want to make major or higher rank," says Larsen, "you have to do your time as an artillery battery commander." It was while serving as the head of a unit of 120 soldiers and a nuclear-capable Howitzer tank that Larsen happened on an unconventional understanding of accountability that molded his every future move in business. "Once a year battery commanders are given a rigorous field test," he says. "Months of planning go into building the team, constructing strategies, and determining exacting maneuvers. If your unit fails the test, you're finished as a commander . . . done and out!

"When a commander fails," Larsen says, "there's *no* excuse because it was their job to get the unit ready. There's no such thing as saying, 'My first sergeant didn't get the paperwork done,' or, 'My forward observer didn't call locations effectively.' The commander is supposed to train a well-coordinated unit with high morale and they alone are accountable for whatever happens."

As the war in Vietnam was winding down, Larsen ended up spending most of his years of service at Fort Carson. Newly married and with the prospect of a Korean assignment, he gave the army notice of his intention to leave.

"I truly enjoyed my time in the military," says Larsen, whose erect posture and carriage give him away as a former officer. "I derived great pleasure out of the camaraderie with the troops and the leadership training I received. The training you receive in the military might not have a business edge to it but it certainly teaches you how to build a team and put together a mission and accomplish it."

Larsen's next stop was Purdue University and an intensive graduate program designed for engineers who wanted to earn an MBA.

Larsen's wife Susan worked as an office manager to keep the young family financially afloat while he worked on classes and papers seven days a week so he could complete the program in one year.

Something one of his professors said near the end of the program had a profound effect on Larsen and has remained with him his entire career. "All the students were interviewing and receiving offers from companies like Ford, GE, and GM," he says, "and one day this forty-year-old strategic management professor (who we thought was ancient) gazed at the class and said, 'I don't understand any of you. You're allowing yourselves to go the highest bidder when you should be doing whatever you want to do. If you want to jump in a car and head to California,' he said, 'do it now. If you want to start a business this is the time to do it, because,' he warned us, 'the older you get and the more responsibilities you have, the fewer options you'll have.'" Larsen considered leaving Goodrich on numerous occasions during his lifelong career there but each time he came close, he remembered the words of the professor, thought about his wife, family, and commitments and decided to stay.

Larsen received a number of job offers but accepted the one from BF Goodrich. "They hired me as an operations analyst," he says, "and my first assignment was analyzing the company's foreign currency transactions. I remember working late at night at home and telling my wife, 'This might be a short job because I have no idea what I'm doing.' My saving grace," he says, "was that nobody else knew either and I somehow managed to get through it."

The next year Larsen was promoted to senior analyst and the year after that promoted again to the level of director. "I suddenly realized I was heading in the wrong direction," he says. "I didn't have a CPA, would never be the CFO, and it was driving me crazy doing all this analysis and never seeing the fruits of my labor." Larsen explained his frustrations to his boss who agreed to move him into the company's tire group as director of planning and analysis, but his new position turned out to be as frustrating as his previous job, because he wanted to make the decisions, not just make recommendations. Larsen went to his boss and said, "I need to do something else, I want to be in the marketplace."

His boss set up an appointment with the SVP of marketing who gave him a job in charge of product marketing for new products where Larsen enjoyed four successful years before deciding it was time to leave the company. "Our tire business wasn't growing," he says, "and the only way to get promoted was if somebody left or retired. We'd also merged our tire business with Uniroyal, which meant there were two of everything and that huge layoffs were imminent, so I polished my résumé and started sending it out."

Before Larsen was able to interview with other companies he caught a career-boosting break when he received a call asking if he was interested in a job as assistant to Leigh Carter, the president of the BF Goodrich Company. At the same time, Dave Burner, the CFO of BF Goodrich Aerospace, who would eventually become CEO, wanted Larsen to run a small aerospace division. Larsen ended up taking both jobs and says it was the best time of his career.

"I had an office where I worked as Leigh Carter's assistant, another a few minutes away where I ran the small aerospace distributing division reporting to Dave Burner, and within a few months we purchased the factory, so I ran it as well," he says. "I was running an entity and it was one of the best experiences I ever had." In the next few years, Larsen ran the company's aircraft tire business and then its evacuation slide business before being promoted to one of three group vice presidents responsible for the aerospace business. In 1995, he became president and COO of the aerospace division and, during his reign, revenues in aerospace grew from $1 to $4 billion and essentially became the company when the industrial group was spun off to shareholders as a separate entity. During the time he ran the aerospace group, Larsen says that Dave Burner largely let him run his own show, which prepared him to eventually become the company's CEO. Larsen's dream came true when he was named

COO of Goodrich in 2002 and CEO in 2003, twenty-six years after joining Goodrich.

Hit the Ground Running

Larsen says that while the operational experience he'd gained during his career at Goodrich prepared him for the role of CEO, he still woke up the morning following the announcement fully feeling the weight of his new responsibilities. "It's a seven-day-a-week, twenty-four-hour-a-day job, juggling lots of balls," he says, "because as the CEO you're responsible for everything that happens in the company."

When Larsen took over as CEO, he had a full plate. The company had gone through a tough time following 9/11. There'd been massive layoffs, two years of no growth, a stock price that had hit an all-time low, and very bad morale because everybody's stock options were underwater with no fresh air in sight. Larsen had a lot of things to fix and get right and had no choice but to hit the ground running unless he wanted to be taken over by another company. Here are the things he did to reverse Goodrich's fortunes and set them on the right trajectory.

Set an Example of Accountability

After studying more than 100,000 companies for my past books, I'm convinced that if you stop and take a deep breath, all companies have a smell. Some reek of incompetency while others give off the distinct aroma of achievement and accomplishment. The satisfying scent in the air at Goodrich is top-to-bottom accountability. It's actually palpable. The company is filled with purpose-driven people who share the same objectives, understand their role in the achievement of them, and efficiently and enthusiastically go about getting done what they've agreed needs doing.

Everyone in business knows that when you're accountable you are responsible for the results. But as front-line managers climb the ladder and become leaders of other leaders, clear lines of responsibility get diffused. Top executives find they have to lead through layers of managers far below them on the organizational chart while still being accountable for the total group's performance. As an executive goes up the chain of command, being accountable gets a lot more complicated.

Some deal with the pressure of accountability by becoming micromanagers—breathing down everyone's neck and making their subordinates nervous and hesitant. Others become finger-pointers; when things don't go as hoped they throw their people under the bus like the *Fortune* 500 CEO who told financial analysts after a miserable quarter, "I gave my people too much responsibility. From today forward I'll be getting my mitts on the details and doing less delegating." (In other words, don't blame me, my team dropped the ball.)

Setting a personal example of accountability is where many leaders fall short. Instead of starting by being accountable themselves, they use the *threat* of accountability as a tool to drive others. They eagerly tell the sales manager she's going to be accountable for revenues. They tell production managers to get the goods out the door on time and marketing managers to create demand . . . or else. Then, under the guise of making everyone accountable, when sales fall short, production snafus occur, and demand isn't there, the leader throws those being held accountable to the wolves. The real question is: What was top leadership doing and what were they accountable for other than holding others accountable?

This is where Marshall Larsen separates himself from the pack. He doesn't micromanage before the fact or point fingers after. West Point and Ranger leadership principles taught him to use each team member with an understanding of his or her capabilities and limitations and to apply all his skills to delegating intelligently and developing subordinates to go willingly and confidently perform their assignments. "Build your team, trust your team, and set the example yourself" are Ranger principles for being a truly accountable leader.

It's far easier for the leader to expect accountability (moving faster in the process) from others when they're prepared to be held accountable. It sends a clear message of "we do what we say we're going to do" top to bottom throughout the entire organization.

Don't Assume

You'll recall that Rule #3 for hitting the ground running is asking for help and getting people on your side. Because Larsen (and outgoing CEO Dave Burner) both served on the board of directors of Goodrich, it would have seemed reasonable to assume that Larsen already knew what the board expected of him in his new role as CEO. But because he understands real accountability, Larsen never assumes anything.

Accountable leaders know that their job is to make sure that what's expected happens. This responsibility depends on having a crystal clear understanding of exactly *what is expected*. Anytime you assume you know what is expected without verifying each expectation, you put yourself at risk. That old saying about the word "assume" is especially true when you're accountable to boards of directors.

But when he became CEO, Larsen knew that if he was going to hit the ground running, he needed to know what board members expected from him. "Because we don't keep outgoing CEOs on the board," says Larsen, "it was a perfect time for me to meet with the eleven outside members of the board individually, find out what they *really* thought was going on with the company, learn what they were uneasy about, and determine exactly what their expectations were of me." In doing so Larsen received solid advice, good counsel, got a clear idea of what was expected of him, and bought enough time to build and implement an agenda.

Pull Together *Your* Team

Most of the CEOs you've read about largely kept their company's senior leadership team in place when they took over, but Larsen felt something was missing that was absolutely necessary if he was going to be accountable. So he decided to make some changes. Remember, Larsen had been with the company for twenty-six years when he became CEO, knew the capabilities of the key players, and already possessed the tribal knowledge that's critical for achieving success.

"My predecessor and I didn't always see eye to eye on who was good and who wasn't," he says. "When I took over, the leadership team was very senior, many had been here too long, believed they knew what was possible and what wasn't, and some had a tendency to be yes-men. I replaced some of them with people who wouldn't be afraid to look me in the eye and tell me I'm wrong."

Experts who study executive decision making in large organizations have learned that there are a couple of factors that help make top executives clueless. The first is the yes-man. Yes-men delay bad news and filter out signs of trouble and warnings from middle managers who tried to report problems. So by the time CEOs see anything is wrong, the problems have grown into near disasters.

Another factor that leads to cluelessness is the behavior of the CEO. During one of our interviews with a CEO, he described his predecessor as having been "seldom wrong but never doubted," and asked that we refrain from attributing the remark to him. It's a great line and fitting description for many charismatic and mercurial CEOs. Some of these larger than life CEOs have a harsh interpersonal style that kills any messenger who comes forward with bad news. This encourages subordinates to conceal or be less than honest when reporting unpleasant facts. It's a tribute to Larsen and his recognition that real accountability requires a complete and true picture of reality so that he could see the incredible value of surrounding himself with people who'd say so when they saw things differently than he did.

"The one thing I did know," Larsen says, "is that if all the leaders in the company thought like me and acted like me, we'd end up with groupthink* and make one hell of a big mistake someday and march off the side of the cliff like lemmings." In typical self-effacing fashion Larsen adds, "I'm not at the top of the IQ list and don't have a corner on all the good ideas. The last thing I want is to have someone tell me what I want to hear."

Select a Specific Destination

"As soon as I became CEO," says Larsen, "I took about twenty people away for a several-day retreat and asked the question, 'Who do we want to be and where are we heading?'" Larsen is quick to point out that he didn't take all the senior leaders of the company to the retreat in the Blue Ridge mountains. "I didn't want the naysayers," he says. "I only wanted the best minds in the company, those people who I knew would be vocal and contribute." Larsen also sent a message to those not asked to attend that it was probably time to dust off their résumés.

"By the end of the meeting," says Larsen, "we'd agreed we wanted to become the world's top aerospace company in terms of return

---

*Groupthink is a phenomenon that can occur when a group of people gathers to make a decision. Essentially, the desire for group cohesiveness and a quick decision clouds the judgment of the people in the group, leading to a decision that frequently fails to deliver the expected results.

on invested capital [ROIC].* "In order to accomplish that objective there were three things we had to do," he says. "We needed to achieve balanced growth (so that, if and when, one market sector was down the impact to the company would be minimized), leverage the enterprise (taking advantage of its size and breadth), and the third," he says, "was operational excellence."

None of the CEOs we studied used the word *vision* to explain where their company was or is headed. The word *vision* has become a buzzword defined as any word used more to impress than inform. When CEOs wax poetic about their visions, as though they're omniscient or channeling spirits, they always miss the rolled-up eyes and smirks of people who've had the vision thing perpetuated on them too many times. Seasoned workers know that visions are vague, ambiguous, and largely unaccountable. Larsen involved his team in the creation of a destination that was real and clear, one that people could get their heads and hands around, go after, and hold each other accountable for reaching.

Put Together *Your* Plan

Accountability is a two-edged sword. You can't ask people to be accountable without giving them the authority to make changes and the resources to execute without unnecessary obstacles. One of the most common obstacles facing new leaders is an old way of doing things.

"Under my predecessor," Larsen says, "Goodrich was completly decentralized. We had eighteen seperate business units, each had its own P&L, and it looked more like a holding company than an operating company." Absolute decentralization undoubtedly worked for

---

*ROIC is a measure of how effectively a company uses the money invested in its operations. It's calculated by dividing net income after taxes by total assets less excess cash minus noninterest-bearing liabilities.

a time, but in Larsen's mind that time had passed. "While I was COO," he says, "I tried to do some things that would take advantage of our size but failed to get any support." This wasn't because his plans were bad but instead it was a matter of decentralized unit heads protecting their turf. As Larsen remembers one his best mentors was fond of saying, "This is no way to run a railroad."

When you're accountable you must take that clear destination and map the best path to get there. One of Larsen's destinations was "leverage the enterprise." He decided that one of the best paths to get there was to centralize HR.

"You can't hit the ground running without talent," says Larsen, "and you can't maintain momentum without developing new talent. When HR teams reported to each business unit, unless they were a big division, they didn't have a chance to develop people. As the CEO, I didn't know who the company's future leaders were."

Larsen asked Jennifer Pollino, who'd been running a half-billion-dollar wheel and brake business, to move to headquarters, set up a centralized HR department, and run it like a business. All the HR teams in the company now report to her, and when management positions in the company are posted, managers are required to consider the full candidate list from all divisions.

Larsen's plan is working. "This method of hiring and promoting ensures that I and the other leaders in the company aren't simply hiring out of expediency or hiring our cronies or people who look like, think like, and act like us. We're truly putting quality people in different positions within the company and giving them direct experience which will insure our continued growth."

Get Total Alignment

"Remember that at the beginning there were only twenty of us who believed in this thing. We simply kept communicating where we needed to be and executed against that plan. We were relentless about drilling deep into the company," says Larsen, "communicating the objectives and working with everyone to make certain their goals and objectives were built to be consistent with the achievement of balanced growth, leverage the enterprise and operational excellence." To put even more meat on the bone, Larsen appointed John Grisik, a well-respected fifteen-year company veteran, as head of a team of experts whose task was to bring operational excellence to the company in manufacturing and supply chain management.

Larsen agrees that destination must become the focus of the organization and everyone must know and understand their role. The acid test of alignment is whether your people can see a clear line between what they do and the goals of the company. In a survey of 12,000-plus executives and front-line employees, almost half said they could not see that line. Goodrich again beats the average company. "We've finally arrived at a place," Larsen says, almost breathing a deep sigh of relief because it was such heavy lifting to get there, "where if you ask anyone in the company what we're trying to achieve you'll find everyone on the same page—they can state our three goals."

Gain Investor Confidence

One of the consistent refrains Larsen heard from members of the board when he held his private meetings with them was that the company had to gain investor confidence. "Frankly, we didn't have any," he says, "but you have to be careful how you go about gaining it. I've seen too many CEOs dig an early grave for themselves by promising Wall Street 15 percent top-line and 20 percent bottom-line growth for the next five years with no basis for making the promise."

Larsen, who takes every promise as seriously as he took his Army officer oath of office, knew he had to have a plan for every promise he made to investors because he would be held accountable for delivering. "The only way I could make promises about our future financial performance," Larsen says, "is if I could develop a mechanism to get the entire company (as opposed to individual business units) moving in the same direction." He says his answer existed in the way people at Goodrich were compensated.

"It's human nature," he explains, "if the business unit you're running is doing well and you've hit your annual objective by September that it becomes easy to coast and buy a bogey for the next year. But when your compensation is tied to how well the entire company performs, you're more likely to keep pushing. When I was out in Phoenix running the evacuation slide business," he says, "I could max out my bonus if I did well, even if the company wasn't performing. That's simply wrong.

"I got the top leaders together," he says, "and explained that the value of their shares and options wasn't based on how well their business unit did but the performance of the entire company and that from that point forward their compensation plans would be directly tied not only to their individual business unit but to the company's overall financial performance. I had to get everyone interested in the entire enterprise."

It comes as a shock to many in business that improved coordination, cooperation, and cross-functional communication are the catalysts for success in today's business instead of dog-eat-dog competition and cutthroat tactics. But not Larsen. "Cooperate and graduate" was a lesson pounded into his head from his first weeks at West Point and it formed the way he runs Goodrich today.

People Philosophy

"At Goodrich," Larsen says, "our people philosophy is simple: We expect everyone to be treated with respect and treat others with respect. For years, American businesses have wasted time making rules for the 5 percent of people who have to be watched," says Larsen, adding, "which is utter nonsense. We work hard to get those '5 percenters' out and have found that our people actually push them out.

"In our San Diego facility," he says, "we had one of our large customers who had a representative on site full time. It turned out he was abusive, didn't respect our people, and was constantly giving them a bad time. One of our managers pulled him aside, told him that Goodrich doesn't tolerate its workers being treated that way, and called his manager and had him permanently removed from our factory. For a while," he says, "we probably didn't have the greatest relationship with that customer but our values are our values and we live them."

Develop an Axis of Advance

Larsen explains that the "axis of advance" is a military term for figuring out where you are (point A) and where you want to get to (point B) and then allowing every level of leadership to develop the plan for how they will achieve their part of the big objective. "You know you have to get to point B. The question is how you'll get there. Along the way," he explains, "there will be unforeseen obstacles and setbacks," and argues that "the best people to build the plan are those closest to the action and more likely to know what they'll encounter.

"Top-down planning doesn't work by itself," he says. "I'd never tell my nine divisional presidents to do it this way or go in that direction. Instead, I'll count on them to tell me how they're going to get there. I want them to put together the strategy and then present it to me.

"Every company faces too many issues for top-down planning to be effective. The person at the top can't possibly know everything there is to know about the competition, supplies of raw material, personnel, engineering, and technical issues. Also, people don't buy into things when they've been ordered to do so by somebody above them," says Larsen, adding, "when people put together a plan they believe in and have bought into, the chances of successfully getting to point B have exponentially increased."

Accountability forces this kind of common sense in planning. Everything ineffective is out when you are accountable. Likewise, you open your eyes to new ideas and new ways when results really matter. It's the perfect medicine to cure dysfunction and inertia in organizations.

Don't Pay Too Much Attention to the Competition

While discussing Larsen's voracious reading habits (a book a week, preferably military themed or history), he revealed another of the basic principles he used to quickly transform Goodrich into an aerospace juggernaut.

Given that he reads so many books annually, I hoped that he'd read some of mine. "Sorry, I have a rule that I don't read any business books," he says, "none at all," followed by a bombshell-sized comment that brought a huge smile to my face. "I don't read any business books," he says, "because I have no interest—zero—I don't want to know what my competitors are doing."

As my coauthor, Laurence Haughton, and I pointed out in our book *It's Not the Big That Eat the Small . . . It's the Fast That Eat the Slow*, too many business leaders spend too much time speculating about the competition and benchmarking themselves to them. Like Larsen says, that's a waste of time. It takes people off their game, prevents them from devoting their full resources to achieving *their* objective, and is only beneficial if part of an argument says, "See, we don't suck any more than they do." Competitive people like Larsen want to win, do their best, and make everyone proud. You're not winning when you limit your goals to just trying to one up your competition.

If a football quarterback dropping back to pass stops to study the 280-pound defensive linemen (the competition) charging toward him, he'll never get his pass off. His job is to get the ball into the hands of the receiver, not study the competition.

Performance

When Marshall Larsen became CEO in 2003, he and his team decided that the company needed to move quickly and achieve balanced growth, leverage the enterprise, and achieve operational excellence. In the five years that he's served as CEO, the company has more than doubled revenues, almost tripled its operating margins, and its three primary market sectors each contribute roughly one third of the company's revenues.

A final example of how strongly Marshall Larsen feels about accountability and how it colors everything he does emerged when he related a conversation he'd had with a good friend. "I was up in the mountains where we have a small weekend place," he says, "and I was talking with a buddy who used to be an executive with MCI WorldCom before he was fired by Bernie Ebbers. The verdict in Ebbers's trial had just come down and he'd been sentenced to twenty-five years in prison for the things he'd done at the company. I told my friend that it seemed like a harsh verdict, that we don't even sentence murderers to that much time in prison.

"My buddy looked at me and said, 'What makes you think he's not a murderer?' and he went on to talk about all the people whose lives were ruined, including some who'd committed suicide as a result of Ebbers's destroying their jobs, the company, and their futures. Believe me when I tell you that I take what I do very seriously," says Larsen, "and need to be accountable for leaving this company better than when I took over." Accountability is how Marshall Larsen hit the ground running at Goodrich.

Hit the Ground Running Rule 8
Be Accountable

Marshall Larsen's rules for becoming and remaining an effective leader include:

- Be accountable. Have a personal sense of responsibility for everything that happens within the organization.
- Set the example and then hold others accountable for delivering as agreed.
- Build your team, trust your team, and set the example yourself.
- Have a crystal clear understanding of what's expected of you. Do the same with those who report to you.
- Forget vision statements. Instead, select a specific destination that everyone understands.
- Develop an axis of advance; plan how you are going to reach your destination.

Rule 9: Cultivate a Fierce Sense of Urgency

Keith Rattie, CEO of Questar, has always been intensely competitive and with a fierce sense of urgency about him. "I admit it," he says. "As a kid growing up, whether it was baseball, chess, Monopoly, or whatever, I always wanted to win. It's a quality," he says, with a still boyish grin, "that didn't always ingratiate me to family members and friends."

Rattie's competitive nature probably helped him become his high school class salutatorian with a 3.98 grade point average, but his speed maybe cost him a perfect GPA because the only class he failed to get an A in was . . . driving. "To this day," Rattie says, "my wife won't let me drive the car when she's in it."

When he took the helm of this natural gas giant as CEO, he did so in typical Rattie fashion and hit the ground running. During his tenure revenues, profits, and earnings per share have doubled and the value of the enterprise has skyrocketed fivefold, from $2 to $14 billion. The watchword during Keith Rattie's reign has been *urgency.*

"You must have a sense of urgency—if one doesn't exist, the CEO's job is to create one," says Rattie. "The mind-set needs to be 'We're not as good as we know we have to be.'"

Questar

Questar traces its history back almost ninety years, when a few entrepreneurs looking for oil near Rock Springs, Wyoming, accidentally discovered natural gas. There was no market for natural gas close by, so the partners pulled off the impossible and built a two-hundred-mile pipeline through the mountains using unproven pipeline construction technology in order to deliver the gas to Salt Lake City, Utah. In proving the impossible *possible* the original partners stumbled on what became the Questar business model—lease blocks of federal land, discover natural gas, pipe it back to Utah, and sell it.

Like oil and coal, natural gas is a fossil fuel created from the remains of dinosaurs and plants that lived tens of millions of years ago. It's odorless, colorless, and shapeless; burns hot; and is far more efficient than oil or coal.

Natural gas is primarily composed of methane but may also include ethane (used in the chemicals industry), propane (used for cooking and for powering buses, taxis, and locomotives and for making plastics), and butane (also used to make plastic). Natural gas is used to heat sixty-five million American homes and businesses, and since the 1990s natural gas has also become a major fuel of electricity generation. Because natural gas has lower carbon content than oil or coal, burning it creates 30 percent less carbon dioxide than petroleum and 50 percent less than coal.

The major drawback of natural gas is the high cost of transporting it. Pipelines are the most economical way of getting it from place to place. Natural gas can also be compressed and transported by truck, or liquefied (at great expense) and transported in insulated ships or trucks.

In the late 1970s Questar (then known as Mountain Fuel Supply Company) was exploring for gas in Wyoming and "accidentally" discovered oil. The company argued that the shareholders should benefit from the sale of the oil, while state regulators in Utah believed that the oil should be sold and the proceeds used to lower retail customers' gas bills. It was a huge issue that dogged the company for years and eventually ended up in front of Utah's Supreme Court.

Finally, in 1981, all parties signed a document known as the Wexpro Agreement under which the company agreed to supply gas from its then-existing natural gas properties to Utahans at cost of service instead of market price (guaranteeing the company a certain after-tax return on investment). The company created a new and separate exploration and production company that would not be subject to state regulation. That company, Questar Exploration and Production (Questar E&P), is now one of the fastest-growing natural gas producers in the country.

Questar today remains a fully integrated natural gas company. In addition to the two exploration and production companies (Questar E&P and Wexpro), Questar invests in gas gathering and processing, interstate gas transportation, and storage and retail gas distribution.

Following twenty years as head of the company, and nearing retirement, former CEO Don Cash and the Questar board in 2000 began the search for a successor CEO who would take the company to the next level. In 2001, Keith Rattie was hired as the company's president and COO, with the intent *but no obligation* to name him CEO upon Cash's retirement.

Keith Rattie

Keith Rattie was born and grew up in Aberdeen, Washington. Like its namesake in Scotland, the town is located at the mouth of two rivers and during its heyday was known as "The Hellhole of the Pacific" because of the huge number of saloons and houses of ill repute that served the thousands of loggers and workers in the town's sawmills. By the time Rattie reached high school, the area was largely logged out, the number of sawmills had dwindled to less than a handful, and the town was developing a blighted and rusty look.

Perhaps it was the town's gloominess that caused so many residents to turn to heavy music. Aberdeen is renowned as the town that gave birth to famous grunge and punk rock bands like Kurt Cobain's Nirvana, Dale Crover's The Melvins, Kurdt Vanderhoof of Metal Church, Patrick Simmons of the Doobie Brothers, and Keith Rattie of Salt Lake City. Yep, that's right. Rattie the CEO, it turns out, is a serious student of rock and roll, plays guitar almost daily, and has been known on occasion to jump on stage at company and civic functions, grab a guitar, and join in with a few licks of classic rock and roll.

"Although I didn't see it that way at the time, in hindsight I guess one could say I grew up poor," says Rattie. "My dad was a mailman—and proud of it—while Mom stayed home with us five kids. I didn't have a clue as to what direction I wanted to go when I grew up," he says, "but the one thing I knew from an early age was that I was going to the University of Washington so I could watch my Dawgs play Saturday afternoons in Husky Stadium."

Rattie enrolled at the University of Washington as a political science major and pondered pursuing a career in politics. "It was a time of great social change," he says, "and it seemed like the natural thing to do." By the end of his freshmen year, which Rattie admits was filled with more partying than he cares to remember, his fraternity brothers convinced him to change his major.

"I was getting A's in calculus, physics, and chemistry," he says. "The upperclassmen in the frat saw that and began asking why political science. Eventually, I saw the light, declared my major in electrical engineering, and traded my rowdy nights for bike rides to an empty classroom where I could study until the work got done." Rattie credits the University of Washington as the place where he grew up, learned self-discipline, and learned how to learn.

While he was a senior, the head of the electrical engineering department passed along Rattie's name to a recruiter from Standard Oil. "I didn't have a suit, had never worn a tie, and didn't have any idea how to tie one," says Rattie. "I suspect I didn't make a very good first impression. I went to the interview in an orange shirt, a black tie borrowed from a friend, brown sport coat, bell-bottomed pants, platform shoes, and hair down to my shoulders."

Despite looking as though he'd just stepped out of what Rattie once described as "Sgt. Pepper's closet," Standard Oil (which soon became Chevron) gave him a $1,000 scholarship and offered him a job at its San Francisco headquarters.

"Having lived through the Arab oil embargo in 1973," says Rattie, "I was all caught up in the mid-seventies belief that we were running out of oil and that the enormous amounts of cash the oil companies were generating should be reinvested in alternative energy. Chevron had some fledgling alternative energy ventures under way at the time, so I decided to join them. It was really my own flawed analysis of market conditions and the energy future of the country that led me to go to work in the energy industry."

For the next decade, Rattie worked for Chevron as a project engineer, shuttling across the country from one assignment to another with increasing responsibilities in San Francisco, Louisiana, Houston, Denver, Bakersfield, California (he jokes that his high-achieving daughter Jennifer will forever be marked with the distinction of having been born in Bakersfield—a rather unattractive American city and the frequent butt of jokes by late-night comedians), and finally back to the company's headquarters in San Francisco for a newly created position titled corporate productivity improvement coordinator. Along the way he picked up an MBA from Saint Mary's College in Moraga, California.

"An engineer with an MBA—the worst combination of anal retentive," chuckles Rattie, poking some good-natured fun at himself. "Engineers," he says, "are trained to be curious and inquisitive about things and fix them when they're broken. But the natural inclination of an engineer is to micromanage, which will kill you in business." Rattie didn't earn an extra dime in pay for getting his MBA but says it helped him be more useful in his role as corporate quality improvement coordinator and that the exposure he received in that role led the company to tap his shoulder when it decided to create a new business unit.

"Outside the United States," he says, "Chevron had always been an oil-focused organization. But in early 1990 top management took stock of trends around the world and concluded that natural gas was about to rise to prominence as a clean-burning fuel not just for heating homes but also for electricity generation. The company created a new international gas unit and put me in charge. I remember sitting around a table with my small group, fully aware that I knew virtually nothing about natural gas. Our mission at the time was to figure out what our mission was. It turned out to be an exciting time and the fork in the road that put me on the path to where I am today.

"I eventually became a fanatic when it came to the role of natural gas in global energy markers," Rattie says. "I would start presentations by declaring 'Today, we call it the "oil and gas industry." Within a decade or two, we'll be calling it "the natural gas and oil industry." ' I was absolutely convinced," he says, "that natural gas would emerge as the fuel of the future, that its importance would one day equal that of oil and wanted to reorient my career toward natural gas."

For the next five years, Rattie traveled the world like Indiana Jones on a mission to figure out ways to commercialize Chevron's huge finds of natural gas in such garden spots as Lagos, Nigeria; Luanda, Angola; and Papua, New Guinea. One of the few things he hated missing during his extended worldwide journeys was his beloved Washington Huskies and Rattie even figured out how to catch a nascent satellite signal and watch their 1991 upset win over the Nebraska Cornhuskers while in a hotel in Mumbai, India.

All those long flights around the world gave Rattie lots of time to think, and he eventually came to two conclusions. "First," he says, "outside the United States natural gas isn't a supply-driven business. It's a market-driven business. Natural gas in a place like Angola is useless until you create a market for it.

"Chevron's a great company, so I don't want to sound critical," he says, "but the company spelled natural gas *o-i-l*. They were oil focused and rightfully so. They had one of the largest oil refining complexes in the nation, and the company's business model for decades was to find and produce oil to feed that system. It was a good fit with the company's engineering culture. But making money in natural gas outside the United States required a different skill set."

In 1995, David Arledge, the CEO of Coastal Corporation, one of the largest pipeline companies in the nation, knocked on Rattie's door. "Coastal was already a major player in the domestic natural gas business," says Rattie, "and wanted someone to help get them become a major player in the global arena. Arledge had a sense of urgency—he saw the fundamentals the same way I did. He got it.

"I left Chevron and joined Coastal," he says, "but not long after I arrived, we concluded that it probably made more sense to stick to the company's core capabilities in the United States where we believed demand was set to boom." Recognizing Rattie's talents, Coastal quickly named him head of the company's nonregulated natural gas operations and recruited Chuck Stanley to run the international gas effort.

In early 2000, Coastal announced plans to merge with El Paso Energy. Rattie wasn't sure if he fit the planned direction of the company. "El Paso's business model," he says, "was 'We wannabe just like Enron.' They'd hired a former investment banker with the intent to transform El Paso from a pipeline company to a merchant trader. It quickly became apparent to the new El Paso management team that I didn't get it and wasn't buying in."

Fortuitously for Rattie, within days of the announced merger a headhunter contacted him about Questar's search for a new president and COO. "I was flattered and intrigued by the call from the headhunter," he says, "and became more intrigued as the uncertain future at El Paso became increasingly obvious.

"I met Don Cash for the first time in April 2000," says Rattie, "and I quickly embraced his vision for Questar. He was stepping down voluntarily from a company he was rightfully proud of. He felt he had the right strategy but that asset-based companies like Questar were out of favor on Wall Street in an era of low natural gas prices and fascination with Enron's merchant-trading business model." During Rattie's interviewing process, Questar's shares traded below $10 per share (it traded as high as $70 per share in July 2008). "Because of his frustration," Rattie says, "Don tried diversifying the company into other areas but they weren't working out."

Following several discussions with Cash, Rattie decided he did want the job. "Questar's hidden value," he says, "and what made me willing to uproot high-school-age children and a wife who were very content in Houston was that I knew the company's assets could be exploited in this new world where the prominence of natural gas was just starting to be fully recognized.

"Eventually, I met one-on-one with the board of directors," he says, "was very frank with them, and told them that if they decided they wanted me as COO, with a planned transition to CEO, they should be mindful of two things. First, it would be my intention to push the pedal to the metal in the exploration and production business. Second, I needed the latitude to make changes to the senior leadership team if required. I told them that if that wasn't consistent with their view of where the company should be headed, then I wasn't the right person for the job." Discussions between Rattie, Cash, and the Questar board of directors lasted almost a full year before it was announced Rattie would join the company.

Then in late January 2001 the Federal Trade Commission approved the Coastal–El Paso merger. "I was an employee of El Paso for about five minutes. As soon as the merger was approved, I called Cash, accepted the job, resigned from El Paso, went home, packed my bag, headed to the airport, and went to Salt Lake City." As it turned out, Rattie's instincts were right. El Paso's planned strategic direction flopped.

Rattie had never run a publicly traded company before and the board of directors had three concerns: Would he earn Wall Street's respect and credibility? Would the existing management team see him as the appropriate person to lead the company? Would the employees accept him?

One key member of the Questar management team did not buy in to Rattie's appointment. "But Don and the board made it clear that I was the person they'd selected and it was up to me to prove my mettle with the investment community and the employees. I came at it from the perspective that I had about a year as COO to be the dumb guy in the room, the guy who would ask the questions that everyone probably had on their mind but were reluctant to ask because a course had already been set."

The big assignment Don Cash gave Rattie when he took over as COO was to spend the year reassessing the corporate strategy. "Don asked me to start with a clean sheet of paper, challenge everything the company had been doing under the existing leadership. He even suggested that we take a hard look at entering electric power and merchant trading," Rattie says.

Rattie says that the investment community had every reason to be skeptical of the COO. But in an attempt to gain Wall Street's respect he borrowed a page from the playbook of two men he considered to be highly successful CEOs. "During my career," he says, "I've had front row seats during two CEO transitions, watching two men who became very successful. Ken Derr, who became CEO of Chevron, and Dave Arledge at Coastal both asked the investment community for a frank assessment of their respective companies. I did the same and asked them to tell me what they really thought of

Questar, not what they thought I wanted to hear," Rattie says. "They appreciated being asked and the things I heard validated a lot of the perceptions I was gathering at the company."

On February 7, one day before the opening of the 2002 Winter Olympics in Salt Lake City, Questar's board went into executive session, asked management to leave, and thirty minutes later called Rattie back in and told him he was going to the be company's new CEO.

Creating a Fierce Sense of Urgency

There are several good reasons for Keith Rattie's sense of urgency. First, it's in his nature. ("Somewhere in my DNA I must have the 'I hate to lose' gene.") Second, he's a zealot when it comes to the role of natural gas in energy markets here and abroad. "There may be no greater challenge facing mankind today than figuring out how to meet the energy needs of a planet that could have nine billion people living on it by 2040," he says. "That challenge becomes even starker when you consider that of the six billion people living on this planet today, nearly two billion do not have electricity—have never flipped a light switch. Simply put, my company and my industry must find and deliver the energy that makes modern life possible."

Here are the things Keith Rattie did to hit the ground running at Questar.

Zero Spin

During his time as COO, as the investment community was telling Rattie what they really thought of Questar, other major events were exploding in the energy business. "The world began to learn the truth about Enron and the shenanigans of the other energy companies who tried to copy the Enron business model," says Rattie.

"Almost overnight, CEOs who were once revered as rock stars fell into disgrace.

"If there's a big lesson to be learned from the failures at Enron, El Paso, the Ken Lays and Jeff Skillings of this world," he says, "it's that honesty, humility, and credibility matter.

"Like everyone else prior to Enron," Rattie says, "we [Questar] had a tendency to exaggerate our successes while downplaying the things that weren't working in our corporate communications. I decided that had to change. We were going to look the facts in the eye, and tell the truth—even when it's inconvenient. We began handling conference calls and speaking during investor presentations with the complete truth. No more starting conference calls with 'We had another excellent quarter,' no more self-inflating hyperbole like 'Our league-leading business unit.' We started saying, 'Here's what we did, here's what we said we were going to do, here's what the best are doing, and we're not doing well enough.'" Rattie says that the moment the zero-spin policy was implemented, he sensed a collective sigh of relief on the part of the entire company. People want to work for honest companies.

But honesty is a double-edged sword. Spinning, fudging, and deceiving are time-delaying tactics that can get you enough time to fix things (or to get away) before you're held accountable. Honesty puts everything in real time. Days of reckoning are never postponed and that's enough to make anyone more urgent.

Focus

"This is a natural gas company," says Rattie, "and I used my year as COO building consensus that we had no business being involved with the alternative strategies the company had gotten involved in. Questar had no business being a dot-com wannabe, building secure data centers, and hosting other companies' Web applications. We had no business trying to imitate the energy merchants or the independent power producers. We're a natural gas company. It was amazing to me," he adds, "to watch how invigorating the decision was for people in the company."

Benchmarking research shows that average companies put seventeen times more stuff on their plate than their better-performing competitors. It's just like with people: If there is too much on your plate, you get weighed down and it's impossible to focus. No focus, no urgency . . . just an urge to nap.

Changing Course

"In 2007 we had an internal planning meeting whose purpose was to look ahead," says Rattie. "As preparation for the meeting I went back and looked at all the things we said in 2002 that we would achieve by 2007. Our assessment of the world was generally correct, but a lot of things turned out to be fundamentally different.

"I have no doubt," says Rattie, "that in 2012, when the leadership team at Questar looks back at our 2007 assessment and planning, they'll wonder, 'How could those people have missed so many things?' You have to be open to signals that you need to change course. And that means building the capability to adapt into every part of your business. It's critical," he says, "that you don't get so full of belief in yourself that you don't see those signs."

One of the brightest venture capitalists I ever met told me he tracked the entrepreneurs he turned down as well as those he funded. His reason was the same as Rattie's. "I want to know what I missed. Every success I didn't anticipate reminds me to not get too cocky."

Scenario Thinking

"Despite the fact that we're reporting record profits and cash flow [in July 2008]," Rattie says, "in many respects I'm more uncomfortable today than I was back in 2002 when I became the CEO. The bottom line is that we're not as good as we know we have to be. History is littered with companies who become seduced by their success, led by management teams who start to see themselves as invincible, entitled to success," he says. "Contentedness can be lethal. Markets change, and when they do, the formula for success changes."

Rattie knows that nothing fails like success. It's one of the big reasons why the big companies get eaten by smaller competitors. Big companies lose their urgency in a sea of complacency, bureaucracy, and entitlement.

According to Rattie, "Someone once said that the plan isn't as important as the planning. That describes our approach at Questar. We don't do formalized scenario planning but are constantly engaged in scenario thinking.

"For example," he says, "natural gas prices today are near all-time highs. But what if high energy prices lead to a surge in gas supplies at the same time that plunging real estate prices lead to a severe recession, resulting in lower energy demand? Or what if Congress, in response to concerns about man-made global warming, decides to mandate the use of wind and solar power, while imposing high taxes on conventional forms of energy such as natural gas?"

Rattie says his job is to ask these questions and then critically challenge the answers that his management team comes back with.

Root Out Contentment

The financial success that Questar has achieved has led to another problem for Rattie to deal with in his drive to root out contentment.

"Within the company," he says, "we've got people who have done extraordinarily well in their 401(k)s because of the equity they've been granted. It's not unusual for HR to receive calls asking them to run the numbers and hearing, 'Gee, so if I retired today . . .' There's a danger," he says, "that people in that financial position will become very content with how things are going, which could lead to complacency and the thinking that what we're doing is working and will always work and so why do anything differently in the future. My job, as the CEO, is to work relentlessly to make certain we don't get infected with that type of thinking. I do it by constantly presenting people with new challenges and responsibilities, having lots of one-on-one conversations about how much more we still have to accomplish, and appealing to their desire to remain part of a winning team."

Do Postmortems

"We do autopsies on all the things we say we're going to do but that don't work out," says Rattie. "Two or three times a year, I'll get up in front of the board and tell them, 'Three years ago we told you about a project we were going to do. We did it. We didn't get the results we told you we were going to get; here's why and here's what we're doing to fix the problems.' That was an extremely uncomfortable exercise for anyone to do here when I arrived," he says. "Standing up and holding yourself accountable for the assumptions you made or flawed execution isn't an easy thing to do," he says, "but if you want to build a culture where making mistakes doesn't mean the end of your career (as long as they aren't a result of incompetence), you have to be willing to admit mistakes, fix them, learn from them, and then step over it and move on.

"We did a brutal postmortem on our involvement in the dot-com company we launched and concluded by asking ourselves, 'How could we have been so gullible as to think that a natural gas company could compete in a business completely unrelated to natural gas, that in attempting to do so we could achieve the market multiples that the dot-com companies were achieving back in 1999?'"

The idea that there's going to be a postmortem is like being in the grandstand at a track event and watching a blind javelin thrower. It really keeps you on your toes.

Don't Copy Others

Even with blisteringly honest autopsies, Rattie says, "There's no guarantee a company won't continue making the same mistake again because, very often, the root of the mistakes are human nature. One of the biggest mistakes companies make," he says, "is believing that just because everyone else is doing something and it's working for them that they need to do it, too.

"One of the biggest causes for failure is trying to emulate somebody else's strategy," he says, adding that "the energy industry is notorious for its stampede mentality. The first law of stampedes is that someone always gets trampled. Many companies are no longer with us because of the belief that if everyone else was doing it, they should be doing it, too."

Ask the "Dumb" Questions

Rattie's recipe for urgency includes a surprising ingredient . . . dumb questions.

"A new CEO—for that matter, even a not-so-new CEO—needs to give himself or herself permission to ask the dumb questions," Rattie suggests. "It's amazing how often others sitting around the table have the same question, but are afraid to ask for fear that it's a 'dumb' question."

What Rattie calls dumb questions are questions that put the spotlight on the presumed conditions and underlying assumptions. Rattie today continues to ask about "the way [Questar] allocates capital, the criteria by which [the company] makes investment decisions, and the role of each one of the businesses." These "dumb" questions have helped make the executive brain trust act more urgently at Questar because they exposed faults in their strategy and upended any possible complacency.

Make Them Proud

"When I was starting out at Chevron," Rattie says, "one of the first things I noticed was how much attention people pay to the person in the corner office—what he does with his time, the things he asks about in the halls or on a field visit, and the degree to which he or she evidences a curiosity about how things are going.

"So one of the things that people had to adapt to when I got here was that I get out and walk the halls frequently," says Rattie, "and I don't just go and visit my direct reports. I enjoy walking into the office of people two, three, or four levels down the organization and asking about some part of their business. It's a great way of getting unfiltered information," he says. "It doesn't matter whether you're the CEO or an entry-level accountant, people love being asked how they're doing and what they're doing.

"I had the great fortune," says Rattie, "to have had some great bosses who frequently said to me, 'You've done the slides, and you've done the research, just go ahead and do the presentation.' They knew," he says, "that I probably wouldn't do as well as they would have done and that I might say some things they'd prefer I not say in front of their boss or boss's boss but they let me tell the story of my work and it made a big impression on me. I also had the other kind of boss," says Rattie, "the boss who doesn't give credit, who takes the work of others and reports it as though it's their own."

"I love bringing top-performing people from lower levels of the organization into the board room," says Rattie, "and let them do the presentations and tell their story. It's a great way to develop people—and it's a great way to identify high-potential people."

Look for the Right Kind of Role Models

Keith Rattie is an unabashed fan of Warren Buffett. "I bought Berkshire Hathaway stock so I can receive and read his annual reports," says Rattie. "He's a good role model for people in jobs like mine." While in Omaha, Nebraska, for an industry convention, Rattie and a small group of energy executives hosted a reception with Buffett. Everyone expected Buffett to make a speech, but the so-called Oracle of Omaha instead cut right to the chase: "Welcome to Omaha; what's on your mind?" After a long, awkward pause, someone in the group stepped forward with the first question: "What mistakes have you made, why did you make them, and what did you learn from them?" Rattie says that Buffett grinned and then said, "I'll answer your third question first. I learned that I should have fired the guy [meaning himself] who made the mistakes."

"Buffett was able to cite the failures he'd made with greater clarity, in most instances, than those things which had made him successful. The most amazing thing about Buffett," Rattie says, "is that when Berkshire Hathaway makes a mistake he says it's because he fouled up. But when they do something right he gives the credit to someone else and downplays his role by adding, 'I didn't think doing it was a good idea at the time, so I guess I was wrong again.'"

Everyone—even CEOs—occasionally require a bit of motivation. When you select the right role model, it provides you a moral compass to measure your actions against, provides inspiration to keep on *keeping on* and serves as a reminder of how much work remains to be done. Rattie couldn't have selected a better role model than Warren Buffett because they share the same ethos and gentle and self-deprecating sense of humor and understand the enormity of responsibilities associated with their positions.

Rattie is as humble as his hero Warren Buffett. "When I looked at the list of CEOs and companies you were writing about," says Rattie,

"I said to myself that I was the luckiest CEO on the list. When I took over six years ago prices of natural gas were about to surge, which significantly increased revenues. I came here with a general sense that the company has some good assets in the portfolio but I didn't know how good they were. I truly stepped into a great situation."

The CEO's Time to Leave

"I don't know when it will be time for me to do what my predecessor did and go out and find somebody new to take over," says Rattie. "But I hope I recognize when that time has arrived and hope for the sake of the shareholders and the employees that when I lose the sense of urgency and the belief that we have to be better tomorrow than we are today, that it'll be time to get somebody else in the chair who will bring a new pair of eyes and fresh thinking to the job. When it happens," he says, "it'll be refreshing and invigorating for everyone."

Hit the Ground Running Rule 9
Cultivate a Fierce Sense of Urgency

Keith Rattie truly embodies the aspirations and the high ideals of his generation and never sold out in the interest of achieving fame or fortune. His rules for igniting and maintaining a fierce sense of urgency include:

- Immediately implement a no-spin policy; tell the truth to everyone.
- Get focused and shed business units you have no real expertise in.
- Root out any sense of entitlement and complacency within the organization.
- Do postmortems on everything that doesn't work as well as everything that does.

- Develop your own strategy; don't copy someone else's.
- Give yourself permission to ask dumb questions.
- Make everyone proud and get them to take ownership.
- Find the right kind of role models.
- Stay humble.
- Know it's your time to leave when you lose your sense of urgency.

Rule 10: Be a Fish Out of Water

While I was traveling for the research on this book, I attended Sunday worship services at a large church near a hotel where I was staying in the Midwest. As I watched the pastor greet his parishioners prior to the start of the service, he seemed to be a pleasant and mild-mannered clergyman.

But as soon as he started his sermon, his demeanor markedly changed and in what can only be described as an all-out fire and brimstone assault on business, he proceeded to blame *every* ill of society on "gluttonous" CEOs and the "greedy" businesses they headed. According to him, *every* problem in the universe can be traced directly to them. The longer his sermon continued, the harder the little zigzag vein on his left temple throbbed and I became convinced he was going to stroke out before he finished. I wanted to jump up and say something but chose to pray instead . . . for his sermon to end.

As the service concluded, the pastor made his way to the back of the church and positioned himself to shake hands with his departing flock. I looked for another exit, found none, and realized the only way out of the church meant I'd be greeting and shaking hands with him. I started mentally searching for some charitable way to let him know how misguided I'd found his sermon. But it wasn't to be.

As the line of departing parishioners slowly snaked forward, I heard one person after another saying, "Right on, great message," "You really hit the nail on the head this morning," and, "Thank you for confirming what I've always believed." I was dumbfounded by what appeared to be universal acceptance and enthusiasm for his message.

Do CEOs deserve such a bum rap? Maybe they do because, by and large, they haven't done a very good job of polishing their collective reputations.

In the early 2000s we had celebrity rock star CEOs, many of whom went on to disgrace themselves and their companies and ended up in jail. Scandal after scandal occurred and confidence in business plummeted. At the height of the confidence meltdown a 2002 Golin/Harris Trust Survey reported that two thirds of Americans held CEOs personally responsible for restoring trust and confidence in business and only 30 percent thought they were doing enough.

Did CEOs do enough to restore confidence in business? Apparently not. According to the Edelman 2008 Trust Barometer (released prior to the close financial catastrophe of late 2008), only 20 percent of Americans trust CEOs to do the right thing for their companies and customers.

As a result of the confidence meltdown in the early 2000s, many CEOs simply went into hiding, surfacing only for required quarterly conference calls with stock market analysts. They didn't want their paychecks and leadership styles to face any more public scrutiny than necessary. But some CEOs still relished the limelight and never met a camera they didn't like.

High-profile former General Electric superstar Bob Nardelli became CEO of Home Depot in 2000 and, during a six-year tenure highlighted by his headstrong and domineering rule, the company's share price fell 40 percent. When asked by the board of directors to take a modest, albeit symbolic, cut in his $38 million annual compensation and have future bonuses tied more closely to the interests of shareholders, he refused and walked out the door with a $210 million departure bonus. His style was so imperious that when he started coming under fire, he arranged for no directors to show up for the company's annual meeting and, during the lightning-short thirty-minute session, used a digital timer to limit questions to sixty seconds and then shut off people's microphones.

The American mortgage mess that caused the collapse of scores of once-venerable financial institutions and whose aftershocks will be felt for years in the world's financial markets was certainly caused by the unabashed greed of CEOs.

Real estate agents sold houses to people who couldn't afford them with the promise that the houses would double in value in a year. They wanted their commissions. Unscrupulous mortgage brokers (who probably had to hold their noses) arranged financing for people they knew didn't have a snowball's chance in hell of paying them back. They wanted their piece of the pie. Equally corrupt financial institutions issued the bad mortgages because they wanted their piece of flesh before offloading them at a profit to Fannie Mae and Freddie Mac, which then packaged them up as bundles of securities and sold them off to other equally greedy firms that borrowed trillions of dollars to buy them (with highly leveraged money), believing there'd always be another gullible buyer somewhere down the road.

While there's more than enough blame to go around, the fact remains that the CEOs of the real estate firms, mortgage brokers, banks, quasi governmental agencies, and investment banking firms could have stopped the alarmingly greedy conduct in an instant, but their eyes were fixed only on the short-term profits of their firms, their upcoming humongous bonuses, and negotiating mammoth golden parachutes for when the good times collapsed.

Bear Stearns was founded and led with one goal in mind, the single-minded pursuit of wealth. When the company's hedge funds, which had taken big bets on subprime mortgages, began collapsing,

James Cayne, the company's CEO, failed to take any responsibility and instead began pointing fingers, firing those underneath him, and sold the last of his shares in the company. As the company struggled to stay alive (it didn't), Cayne was absent more than half the time playing golf, competing in bridge tournaments, and, according to the *Wall Street Journal,* smoking ganja at the end of his tournament sessions.

Following a single quarter's $8 billion loss, Stanley O'Neal (another imperial CEO) was forced out as chairman and CEO. It was discovered the company had been making huge bets on the bond market that weren't in compliance with the guiding principles of the company's finance and audit committees. To try to prop up the company, O'Neal floated the idea of a merger with Wachovia without consulting his board of directors. O'Neal's blunders continued to hound the firm long after he'd left in the form of consecutive multibillion-dollar quarterly losses and the necessity to sell the once revered brokerage business at a fire sale price to Bank of America.

When Daniel Hesse agreed to take the job of CEO and attempt to save Sprint Nextel, a company that under former CEO Gary Forsee had become so demoralized and decimated that employees called corporate headquarters "Shawshank" after the prison in the movie *The Shawshank Redemption,* they took bets the company was in such bad shape that the new CEO wouldn't show up for work. Reeling from a botched merger that Forsee had spearheaded, the company had slashed spending on customer service and was losing a million customers a quarter. During his first meeting with company leaders, Hesse asked who was in charge of dealing with unhappy customers and no one raised a hand. In another meeting with the company's finance team he asked who was in charge of creating the firm's earnings projections and no one knew the answer.

Are these just a few isolated cases carefully chosen to set up a straw man, knock him down, and make a point? No. Many more names could be added to the list. According to Transactional Analysis Clearing House (TRAC), an organization that gains access to and analyzes case-by-case information under the Freedom of Information Act, an average of eight to ten thousand white collar prosecutions occur each year, a number only modestly surpassed by weapons prosecutions. It seems there are almost as many business leaders lying, cheating, and defrauding people as there are people using weapons to commit crimes.

Hard-Charging, High-Profile CEOs

In addition to the CEOs who were taken down by greed and headstrong arrogance, there have been a number of high-profile CEOs whose personality traits mirror what most books on management and leadership have led us to believe what strong leaders should be: straight-talking, hard-charging, tough taskmasters.

Robert Crandall, former CEO of American Airlines, earned his reputation for being a tough, hard-charging leader by demanding the front lines at American Airlines be held accountable for customer satisfaction. But his harsh edict for dealing with any employee who dropped the ball—*"Crandall wants to see the corpse"*—caused more problems than it solved, leaving an opening for a competitor—Southwest Airlines—to actually become the flying public's favorite airline. Crandall later advised American's employees not to invest in the company, telling them, "An airline is a great place to work but a horrible investment," and added that "I've never owned any stock in American Airlines or any other airline and urge you to do the same."

Larry Bossidy, former hard-charging CEO of Allied Signal, is on record as telling people they have to go balls to the wall because, according to him, "incrementalism is a sign of a mediocre mind."

When Carly Fiorina, the former steely CEO of Hewlett Packard, well known for her abrasive my-way-or-the-highway manner, was finally fired after halving shareholder value during her six-year tenure, the company's stock price soared because, as one analyst said, "The street had lost all confidence in her and the market's hope is that *anyone* will be better than she was."

Do the requirements for becoming a CEO include having a dictatorial style of rule and the need to always be the center of attention, being imperious in nature and quick to blame others, as well as having a ready willingness to shoot the messenger, unrestrained self-interest, and headstrong arrogance? The priest who gave the sermon to his rapt congregation certainly thinks so, and evidence would point in the direction of two thirds of people believing it, too.

Fish Out of Water

Once the best-performing CEOs in the nation had been identified, but before contacting them and arranging to get their stories, my research team and I started informally interviewing other CEOs and board members we'd gotten to know as a result of previous books and speeches. We asked them what their take was on the CEOs we'd identified and asked for their opinions. Over a period of several months we also contacted competitors, customers, consultants, and almost anyone we could think of who knew them in order to begin drawing a mental image of their personalities and leadership styles.

According to the people we spoke with, many of the CEOs on the list didn't fit the stereotypical mold. People kept referring to them as "humble, authentic, accessible, highly ethical, compassionate listeners and truly committed to doing the right thing for *all* stakeholders." They weren't the kind of bosses Stanford Professor Roderick Kramer lionized in his study of high-performing CEOs titled "The Great Intimidators."

We kept digging and talking to people. Surely there had to be some CEOs who fit the mold of what we've been led to believe CEOs are supposed to be. We weren't disappointed and eventually started hearing about a couple of CEOs who fit the profile of what people believe CEOs to be to a "t."

Our original list of companies included Motorola's then chairman and CEO, Ed Zander, and E*Trade's CEO, Mitch Caplan. Described by various sources as "type A, personally charismatic, and powerful, intense, and regal bearing," it was comforting to know that we'd managed to identify a diverse group of CEOs and that at least two of them fit conventional wisdom. Then, during our research, a strange thing happened. These two CEOs imploded.

Zander had said he was a new breed of CEO. "I want to build on the good things at Motorola," he told David Smith of the *Financial Times*, "with a high commitment to integrity, treating people fairly, and doing the right thing." But insiders, like Numair Faraz, say this was mostly PR spin. Zander was very much old school.

"He engineered billions of RAZR profits into stock buybacks" for short-term gains instead of channeling money into more innovation, writes Faraz. He got the company into big bets on things he didn't really understand like the "ill-fated ROKR" (an iTunes phone). And when results didn't come as promised, he blamed others and tossed them under the bus. "Maybe Geoffrey [the late Geoffrey Frost, champion of the hugely successful Motorola RAZR] should have come up with a better successor," he told Faraz in a 2007 phone call. Unable to produce another blockbuster product, Motorola's stock went into freefall, outside vultures began circling, and Zander stepped down before a rumored firing could occur.

After Caplan repeatedly and publicly stated that his firm had minimum exposure to subprime mortgages, it was revealed that the firm stood to lose billions in those exact investments, the stock plummeted, billions of dollars of additional capital had to be raised, the company came within a hair of bankruptcy, and Caplan resigned in disgrace.

Not wanting to include two CEOs who had either resigned in

disgrace or fallen from grace, we were forced to go back to our original research and replace those two companies with the next two from our original list.

When all the interviews were complete and we began analyzing everything we'd seen and heard it became obvious that the best-performing CEOs in America are an unusual breed—so unusual that we started calling them "fish out water."

TRAITS OF A CONVENTIONAL LEADER VERSUS A FISH OUT OF WATER LEADER	
A Conventional Leader	**A Fish Out of Water Leader**
Does whatever it takes to hit the numbers	Practices the Golden Rule
Is secretive about strategy	Lets everyone know the strategy
Demands employees' belief	Earns belief of employees
Avoids revealing any sign of weakness	Asks others for help
Sees subordinates as dispensable tools	Believes a company's only real competitive advantage is its people
Talks	Listens
Behaves like a politician, going in whichever direction the wind blows	Plants stakes in the ground and rallies people around a noble purpose
Has a plan and implements it	Builds a plan and gains buy-in
Creates cover through complication	Simplifies everything
Is quick to replace the top team	Wins over the existing team
Is imperial	Is accessible

(continued)

TRAITS OF A CONVENTIONAL LEADER VERSUS A FISH OUT OF WATER LEADER	
A Conventional Leader	**A Fish Out of Water Leader**
Does a major transformation	Has an incremental approach to change
Is distant	Is compassionate
Points fingers and places blame	Is personally accountable
Is very sure he or she is right	Doubts his or her own infallibility
Fosters an atmosphere where gossip and palace intrigue rule	Supports transparency between executives and staff
Feels a sense of urgency based on creating personal wealth	Feels a sense of urgency based on making things better for all stakeholders
Hires for experience and credentials	Hires for attitude and character
Is bigger than life	Is humble
Destroys comfort zones	Doesn't push everyone to change
Studies the competition	Studies the customer

The Power of Improved Leadership

At the same time I was researching this book, John Van Reenen (London School of Economics) and Nick Bloom (Stanford University) made a critical discovery. "One of the most effective strategies for outperforming the competition," they wrote in *Management Matters,* "is improving management practice." They led a study of four thousand companies and found direct correlation between improving leadership skills and increasing profitability, productivity, and revenue growth.

Their research (covering eighteen different practices in managing people, processes, and accountability) pegged the value of just one point of overall improvement in leadership effectiveness "as being equal to a 65 percent increase in invested capital."

But the most surprising conclusion of this comprehensive study was that "leadership excellence" is not a strategic priority in most organizations. The majority of executives they interviewed couldn't put their finger on what their company could do better (if anything), nor did they have any plan for improving the leadership tactics used by their managers.

Reenen and Bloom suggest that the difficulty of implementing better practices keeps many firms from doing anything specific.

I think there's an even bigger obstacle that keeps most of today's leaders from achieving their full potential. The world has changed since 2001 and our view of leadership hasn't kept pace. We're stuck on a model—authoritarian, overcontrolling, egotistical, insensitive, and (when put to the test) not completely trustworthy—that has succeeded in the past. And though we suspect that different times call for different leadership, we are slow to let go.

It's Time for a Change

Peter Lynch is undeniably one of the greatest investors in the world. During his tenure in charge of the Fidelity Magellan Fund he grew it from $20 million to $14 *billion,* averaging an annual return of 29 percent. One of his guiding principles has always been that "by the time something becomes obvious to everyone it's too late to profit from it."

My evidence is not obvious but should be compelling. Almost everything we've heard and accepted about being a top-performing business leader is now wrong. Leading a business isn't about greed or doing whatever investors demand, creating a top-notch spin machine, kicking ass, pointing fingers, or viewing employees as necessary irritants.

It's about being a compassionate, empathetic individual, doing unto others as you'd have them do unto you, telling the truth and gaining belief, building and listening to your team, having belief in others, boldly and publicly proclaiming your strategy so that everyone feels a part of what's happening, building cultures that make people feel proud, accepting personal responsibility, and never resting on your laurels as you work relentlessly to make tomorrow better for everyone.

Drive Your Stake in the Ground

The question I'm asked most frequently is about implementation. People constantly ask, "I get what you're talking about, but how can I implement all these things in my business?"

Most people have a fairly good idea of right and wrong and start out wanting to do the right things in the right ways. After all, this book can't claim copyright to the Golden Rule. But, eventually, after having been stymied by ridiculous bureaucracies over and over, having seen too many suck-ups being rewarded by old school leaders, and having stood on the sidelines as distortions and lies got made and told in order to hit the numbers, people give up, go along, and eventually join in.

If you aspire to be a highly successful business leader, the best way to start is by listing your values and then saying, "These principles are stakes I'm driving into the ground and I will not allow them to be violated." Start living them in everything you do. Review the stories of these great leaders frequently. When making decisions, pause and ask, "What would a truly great leader, a fish out of water, do?"

Don't Let the "You Know Whats" Get You Down

Observing outdated, old-fashioned leadership tactics used in other companies is disappointing but it's downright disheartening when you encounter them in your own company or colleagues. And, just like a lush constantly pressuring everyone around them to join the party, people who practice out-of-date leadership techniques will constantly pressure you to cave in, follow conventional wisdom, go along with them, and do things they way they're doing them. They're pushers. Don't buy or use their drugs.

When Marshall Larsen was a cadet at West Point, he had to constantly remind himself that he wouldn't let harassment by upperclassmen get in the way of getting a great education and graduating as an officer. When Pat Hassey was moved from one bad boss to another, he began building a list of the ways he'd never treat people. And when Keith Rattie found himself in the middle of a merger and a business model he seriously questioned, he chose to leave.

You can't change other people but you can change yourself. Instead of concentrating on the fact that those around and above you don't get it, reject their values, tactics, and teachings and begin studying and emulating the authentic values and tactics practiced by America's best new leaders.

My researchers and I began this project with an agenda to figure out what America's best performing business leaders were doing to create value for their shareholders. We discovered something much bigger. We found that the CEOs who have created the greatest amount of economic value for their companies are a new breed of leader with ideals and values. They are good stewards truly committed to helping all stakeholders achieve their full economic potential, making everything better for everyone and making everyone proud.

Are you ready to be a good steward?

120 Quotes from
America's Best-Performing CEOs

Many of the statements made by the CEOs we studied are worthy of remembering. Here are some favorites for your quick reference and use.

The Job of the Leader

"My job as a leader is to root out contentment."

—Keith Rattie, chairman and CEO, Questar

"Listen. Be humble. Doubt your own infallibility."

—Tim and Richard Smucker, cochairmen and co-CEOs,
The J. M. Smucker Company

"To go from good to great, you've got to drive change. It doesn't mean you throw out everything in the culture but you clearly have to have a change in direction."

—Howard Lance, chairman and CEO, Harris Corporation

"The CEO's job is to be a destination expert. The CEO's job is to let everybody know where we are going."

—Pat Hassey, chairman and CEO, ATI (Allegheny Technologies Inc.)

"There must be clarity about why and how you want to become great. Then you have to stockpile the talent and build a sense of entrepreneurship."

—Fred Eppinger, chairman and CEO, The Hanover Group

"Oversimplify everything! Sit down and ask, 'If I could start with a blank sheet of paper today and create the best answer, what would I do?' Write down what you'd like it to look like, and then ask, 'How close can I get?' Maybe you can only get 70 percent of the way there. That's pretty close. You have to get away from the immediate problem to say, 'Where am I trying to get and what would I do if I could do anything I wanted?'

—Jeff Lorberbaum, chairman and CEO, Mohawk Industries Inc.

"You have to figure out the numbers that really matter. Most people don't take the time."

—Mike McCallister, president and CEO, Humana Inc.

"My objective when I leave this job is to leave this business in the best shape it's ever been for my successor. I want them to be looking ahead much more than I was in the first few years, when I was busy fixing things and shoring up to make sure we could move ahead."

—Marshall Larsen, chairman and CEO, Goodrich Corporation

"You have to communicate what you're doing. If people don't know what's going on, they'll think nothing's going on."

—Ron Sargent, chairman and CEO, Staples, Inc.

Finding and Keeping the Right People

"I play the players I have. I'm not one of those people who take on a new situation believing I have to sweep the place clean and completely change everybody."

—Mike McCallister

"People come first on our list of basic beliefs. We will always be fair with our employees and maintain an environment that encourages personal responsibility. In return we look to them to be responsible for their jobs and for the company as a whole."

—Tim and Richard Smucker

"You can't be embarrassed by the company you're with and you have to believe that you're going to win."

—Fred Eppinger

"People never quit a company; they quit their boss."

—Pat Hassey

"People are either on the train or they're not on the train and if they're not taking the train, they have to get out of the station."

—Ron Sargent

"I'm a big believer that centers of influence matter in an organization and that you'll never know where they are by looking at an organizational chart. They're embedded in places that are amazing and you need to find them and make sure they get it."

—Mike McCallister

"Everybody wants to know how they fit, what the boss wants them to do and they want success to be defined. If you can answer those questions from the top guy all the way down to the bottom guy, you've got a team that won't be beaten."

—Pat Hassey

"It's very much about listening. Listening brings involvement, involvement brings understanding, and understanding brings commitment."

—Howard Lance

Dos and Don'ts

"Don't trust what people tell you without verifying that they really know what they're talking about."

—Mike McCallister

"You have to constantly remind yourself—and your people must believe—that you're not nearly as good as you have to be to be successful. That can't be just a clever play on words but the way you conduct business as an organization."

—Keith Rattie

"You've got to be brutally honest about what you know and what you don't know."

—Keith Rattie

"Don't make rules for the 5 percent of people who don't comply. We want to get those people out of the organization. Actually, the good people eventually push them out."

—Marshall Larsen

"We take care of our suppliers. We can't pressure our suppliers so much that they don't make any money. If we do, we won't have long-term growth, long-term good-quality suppliers."

—Tim and Richard Smucker

"You never get a second chance to make a first impression."

—Howard Lance

"There are still a lot of imperial CEOs who are impressive and personally powerful but that's often superficial. Workers see a lot more than they're given credit for. They know if you're genuine. And they know if it's all about you or if it's about *us*."

—Howard Lance

"I always operated as though I was the final decision maker on everything. If you're going to ask people to follow you and see you as the leader you have to take accountability and responsibility for everything. The minute they think the decisions are coming from somewhere else or it isn't your idea, you're toast."

—Mike McCallister

"You have to clearly articulate the potential and then have people believe that the organization isn't operating at full potential."

—Howard Lance

"You could get tempted to bend the numbers. It's not worth it. I'd rather be fired for not producing."

—Marshall Larsen

"It is easy to grow if you stay focused doing the same thing repetitively and minimize complexity."

—Jeff Lorberbaum

"The worst bosses I had were the ones who managed their job to get information from their people so they could report it upwards as their own."

—Keith Rattie

"Don't stay too long. Business changes, life changes, and markets change and businesses need a fresh set of eyes."

—Howard Lance

Culture

"Leaders need to make explicit the connection between ethics and culture. We don't believe in business ethics. We believe in ethics, pure and simple. It's how they're applied to all walks of life that matter. Ethics is doing what's right even when no one is looking."

—Tim and Richard Smucker

"People don't work for companies just to earn a paycheck. They want to feel good about the companies they work for and they want to feel like they're making a difference in the world."

—Ron Sargent

"There are seven hundred insurance companies in the world. Nobody needs another because most of them aren't great. I got up in front of our people and told a story of how we could become world class. I call it the journey. The story has never changed and never will change until they drag my ass out of here."

—Fred Eppinger

Tips on Strategy, Planning, and Buy-in

"The plan isn't nearly as important as the planning."

—Keith Rattie

"I asked a lot of dumb questions. Dumb questions change an operation and make it better."

—Pat Hassey

"We quit focusing on our competition. I told everyone that I didn't want any effort and energy focused on the outside; I wanted it all on the inside."

—Ron Sargent

"I need everyone to respect and support one another and work with each other. Everything else is B.S."

—Fred Eppinger

"People don't buy into things when they're ordered to do. They buy into things when they participate and are part of the process of coming up with where they're going and how they're going to do get there."

—Marshall Larsen

"The numbers usually work; it's the drudgery of implementation where companies fail."

—Keith Rattie

"Define the small steps you can take. Take a step, and then reevaluate the end game. Hopefully, you're not off too far, but if you are, adjust the steps as you take them. Break everything it into small pieces and start with one piece at a time."

—Jeff Lorberbaum

"You have to carve out a coalition of the willing—those who will take a chance, who want a new experience, and who want to grow. Then make sure that everyone else has important work to do but let them stay in their comfort zone. Everybody doesn't have to be pushed to the limit. Cull out the subset of people who are willing, because they're the ones who will drive change and take the company to the next level. Some people not only don't want to do it, but they wouldn't be very good at it."

—Howard Lance

"Profit is a by-product of doing what's right. And if we really do what's right, the profit will be there."

—Tim and Richard Smucker

"You have to be open—completely open—to signals that tell you that you need to change. That means building the capability in every part of your business to adapt to a world that turns out to be different than the one that you assumed and not getting so full of your own belief and *your* plan that you don't see those signs."

—Keith Rattie

Creating Urgency

"Time is the differentiator. Everyone has the same amount. It's how you use it to create a competitive advantage that's the key."

—Howard Lance

"You always have to have a sense of urgency. Sometimes the sense of urgency is driven by results that are not acceptable. Other times, it needs to be driven by the fact that the world is going to change and nobody knows what those changes are going to be. You have to strive to be prepared and that means constantly becoming better at the fundamentals."

—Keith Rattie

"It has to do with never being satisfied, what I call constructive dissatisfaction. It's at the moment of victory that you can be sowing the seed of your future defeat. After you jump the bar, you've got to raise it. Go back and do it again. That's who I am as a person and what I aspire to be."

—Howard Lance

Mistakes

"We all make mistakes. Just don't keep making the same ones."

—Marshall Larsen

"I want the bad news first and I'm not going to shoot the messenger that brings it. I just want to know the truth. The best thing anyone can do is tell me the truth."

—Pat Hassey

"I can work with people who make mistakes. I can't work with people who don't live by our values: ethics, openness, trust, proper dealings with our customers, accountability, and teamwork.

—Marshall Larsen

"Sometimes you have to admit your baby is ugly. That's just the way it is! We're moving fast, we're going to make mistakes. Your baby's ugly. You just have to say it. Okay?"

—Fred Eppinger

"You try to minimize mistakes. You try to take the risks that won't hurt you. Make them short and sweet, throw some money at them, and if it doesn't work, go on to the next one. It's okay to lose the occasional battle . . . but never risk losing the war."

—Jeff Lorberbaum

"Why bother trying to affix blame? Instead, ask how we're going to do something to fix it, make it better and turn the situation into a positive, and ask what we've learned. I learned a long time ago that it doesn't make any sense looking for someone to shoot. It doesn't help anything."

—Pat Hassey

The First One Hundred Days

"In most turnarounds, what you do is you take the three things that are really good and overinvest on those and underinvest or get rid of the bad things."

—Fred Eppinger

"Whenever I took over a hospital I'd tell the maintenance staff to start painting doors. Why? Because I want the smell of paint in the building to let people know things are going to change and get better. If a place looks like a dump, people are going to think it's a dump."

—Mike McCallister

"Always pick the biggest piece that's killing you and fix it first."

—Jeff Lorberbaum

The Customer

"My first day as CEO I put on the Red Staples shirt and worked in the store. I did it because of the importance of the stores, our customers, customer service, and the importance of the people who are dealing with our customers every day. If the CEO thinks customer service is vitally important, it'll happen. Making customers our number one priority was as important as anything we've ever done."

—Ron Sargent

"The idea of aligning your business with your customers is as natural as breathing. I wouldn't know how to do it any other way."

—Howard Lance

"Customers don't care as much about price as they so about merchandise being in stock, quick in, quick out, fast checkout, and knowledgeable, friendly people."

—Ron Sargent

"Find out what your customers want and give it to them. It's not hard."

—Jeff Lorberbaum

Dealing with Your Investors

"I've seen other CEOs go out and say they're going to grow their company at 15 percent top-line, 20 percent bottom-line growth for the next five years without any basis for saying it. That's a wish for an early grave."

—Marshall Larsen

"No spin. Look the facts in the eye and tell the truth."

—Keith Rattie

"Investors who want to come into this company and grow with us will have a great opportunity. Maybe the horizons are eighteen to thirty-six months at a time. It's not a quarter-to-quarter thing. People that try to keep the quarter-to-quarter investors happy won't adequately invest in the capital assets of the business."

—Pat Hassey

Finding Other Great Leaders

"The CFO, the head of HR, and the general counsel were sixty, sixty-one, and sixty-three and assumed I'd put them all out to pasture. Well, I didn't put any of them out to pasture. Why would I have done that? They had the tribal knowledge of this place."

—Howard Lance

"Leadership is the art of building and sustaining a high-performing organization. It's not about the CEO getting credit. It's about making your organization more than it is."

—Howard Lance

216

"I know something about the top 250 people in our company. They are the ones who will determine if we're successful. I need their loyalty but also want to understand them so I can help get them in their job. You can't change anything with those people without my personal approval. You can't change their job. You can't change their compensation. You can't change their title. You can't fire. You can't do anything with that group."

—Howard Lance

"If you're going to build the best insurance company in the world you're going to have to attract and retain the finest people so only people who care about developing other people can be here. You can't pull a switch and all of a sudden have a following."

—Fred Eppinger

"One boss I had didn't have thirty years of experience; he had five years' experience six times."

—Pat Hassey

Learning to Lead

"Leadership is about people believing in something that they can't necessarily touch or feel."

—Howard Lance

"First, say thank you for a job well done, listen with your full attention, look for the good in others, and have a sense of humor."

—Tim and Richard Smucker

"Business is about getting results. And you can do that a lot more effectively if you get more people on your team."

—Howard Lance

"Always hit your numbers and you'll always be loved."

—Mike McCallister

"People should want me to ask them to go and work somewhere outside the United States. Everybody should want to do that. It will be a life-changing experience, and it will be lot more positive than negative."

—Howard Lance

"Everyone should write a retirement speech including what they want to accomplish, the way they want to be remembered, and the impact they want to have in life. When I wrote mine I learned that I wanted to be remembered as someone who built and inspired a team of people who grew as individuals, be a respected voice of the company within the community, and be someone who'd earned the right to lead. I didn't just want to be a successful CEO who'd made the shareholders and himself a lot of money."

—Howard Lance

"The first hospital administrator I worked for knew everybody in the building by their first name, including the person mopping the floors, and he showed every one of them incredible respect. That builds an awful lot of goodwill and a foundation where people have an inclination to want to help."

—Mike McCallister

Long Term Versus Short Term

"The short-term stuff favored by so many CEOs will kill you. I'm not building this for a quarter. I'm not building this for a decade. I'm building a world-class company that's going to be the envy of this industry when you look back in ten years."

—Fred Eppinger

"When you see all these one-hundred-year-old companies dying it's because somebody came in, changed its culture, changed its value structure, did whatever it took to go for the short term, and they died."

—Pat Hassey

"Any decision that I've ever made that maximized the short term I paid for in the long term. You might as well do it right the first time because the problem will just get bigger. Face whatever the damn cost is to fix it and get it done because it only gets more expensive to fix it if you postpone it."

—Jeff Lorberbaum

Making Good Decisions

"One of the biggest causes for failure is trying to emulate somebody else's strategy. Many industries are known for having a stampede mentality. The first law of stampedes is that somebody always gets trampled."

—Keith Rattie

"Never make compromised decisions. When you get to a compromise, you've already lost something. There is *always* a right answer that is the closest to what you should be doing."

—Pat Hassey

"Sometimes when you win, you lose, and sometimes when you lose, you win."

—Marshall Larsen

"Sometimes you simply fall into things, but you'd better be prepared to recognize what you've fallen into."

—Jeff Lorberbaum

"I worked for a guy once who told me he believed that companies with a good heart got a lot of help from above. If you're doing the right thing, have a good heart, and it's good for humanity, the ideas will come and the markets will open up. I believed him."

—Pat Hassey

The Recipe for Success

"It's very much about listening. Listening brings involvement, involvement brings understanding, and understanding brings commitment."

—Howard Lance

"Accountability. Period. As a battery commander I knew if I failed the annual field test I'd be finished as an officer."

—Marshall Larsen

"Our real secret is our hiring. We look for attitude before aptitude and for character before credentials."

—Tim and Richard Smucker

"I like being surrounded by people who aren't afraid to look me in the eye and say, 'I don't agree with you. You're wrong.' If everybody agrees with me on everything, one day we'll all march off the side of a cliff."

—Marshall Larsen

"People always talk about how difficult it is to terminate somebody. I agree that it's difficult to terminate somebody, but I think you've got a choice: You can either sacrifice a job or a handful of jobs or risk sacrificing all the jobs."

—Ron Sargent

"I like to know what's true. There are systems that don't tell you all the truth all the time. You can't afford to have them in your company."

—Pat Hassey

"Any CEO who thinks he pulls all the strings that make things happen is kidding himself."

—Marshall Larsen

"If you don't have the passion and the commitment to go at something with tenacity, you're not going to be very happy."

—Marshall Larsen

"If it doesn't feel right in your gut, you shouldn't be doing it. If it feels right and you know its right, then you should be doing it."

—Pat Hassey

"When someone preaches something and doesn't live it, it's hollow. We'd rather just live our values on a day-to-day basis."

—Tim and Richard Smucker

"Many companies make a best guess at where they want to be and take a step that's far too big. The troops can't follow it, people can't execute it, they lose sight of the customers, and they get themselves to a point where their assumptions are completely different than reality. They screw it up."

—Jeff Lorberbaum

"I always feel better when I get back here after having been out in the field. If you spend all your time in headquarters, you'll go crazy because you're only talking to twenty people and everything is filtered."

—Mike McCallister

"I'm trying to get to the top of the mountain. What do I give a damn if I end up on top of the next one? I don't care which one it is. The view is nice from any of them. But some people pick one mountaintop and they won't let go."

—Jeff Lorberbaum

"I'm never going to stop learning. I'm never going to stop expanding. And I'm never going to be satisfied. I want to prove that our growth and what we've accomplished is sustainable and not some flash in the pan that happened when the stars aligned and we were great for five years."

—Howard Lance

"It doesn't help to hide any of your problems, so you'd better always be honest with people, especially the people who have the most ability to help you."

—Mike McCallister

"Quit reacting to competitors. Decide what you're going to do well and go after what you do well instead of reacting to the competition."

—Jeff Lorberbaum

"I've found that adaptability—often thought of as a soft trait—has a lot to do with being successful."

—Howard Lance

"I'm in stores every week—hundreds a year—because you'll get a straighter answer from someone stocking shelves than from somebody who's an executive vice president of whatever. Firsthand knowledge of what's going on is vital."

—Ron Sargent

"Follow your gut instincts. Have a big heart. Know what you're doing. Know the business you're in. Know what your skill sets are and hire people to make up for your shortcomings. Have good people around you that can help you. Then, put your shoulder to the wheel and say, 'Let's go!' "

—Pat Hassey

Morale

"No one will be engaged unless they believe that their boss cares about them. It's impossible."

—Pat Hassey

"We try to treat all of our people like they are adults, which sounds like straightforward common sense, but it's amazing how many businesses don't."

—Mike McCallister

"We're all here for one purpose, all the way down to Paul, the guy who drives the company shuttle. In my world, he's as important as anybody else. If any of my executives treat him differently than me, they're in deep *bleep*."

—Fred Eppinger

What Keeps You Awake at Night?

"A lot of company's start to drink their own Kool-Aid. Once they've had a little bit of success they start to think that the things that led to success in the past will guarantee their success in the future. They start believing they're entitled to be successful. That's a huge vulnerability."

—Keith Rattie

"Complacency and bureaucracy keep me awake. Our dream is to be the world's best office products company. Occasionally when somebody says, 'Well, we already are,' I become very worried. We're not there yet."

—Ron Sargent

"What happens in a lot of companies is they become very distant, very big, very bureaucratic, and hierarchical. If you either fool yourself or encourage people to not tell you when bad things happen, the whole thing can blow up."

—Fred Eppinger

"When corporate staffs become more engaged with oversight than they are in enabling growth, there's trouble ahead. Everyone must know theirs is a role that in some way serves customers and they must strive to be faster and nimbler at doing it."

—Howard Lance

"If you're not growing and evolving, eventually you are going to wither and die."

—Mike McCallister

My Heroes

"I admire leaders for more than just a result. I admire them for how they get it. I admire them for what they do outside of work or who they are in their community and with their family."

—Howard Lance

"Warren Buffet can cite his failures with greater clarity than his successes."

—Keith Rattie

"My father went to work every day and came home every day covered in grease from head to toe and my mother ran the household and made sure that we got to school and grew up right. Those core early values stay with you. Hard work, respect for people, honesty, integrity, and education are all vitally important."

—Ron Sargent

Why I Do What I Do

"We believe in the goodness of mankind, that people want to do the right thing and that values do make a difference."

—Tim and Richard Smucker

"I am trying to change the world of health care."

—Mike McCallister

"We've created 74,000 jobs. When you think about the houses those jobs have purchased and the children they've put through college, it can bring tears to your eyes. The good that comes from running a big business and doing it well is what makes it worthwhile."

—Ron Sargent

"We take care of people when something horrible happens. That's the important work we do."

—Fred Eppinger

"I believe this country needs investment. I believe that people need good jobs. I believe that the manufacturing base provides good jobs. I believe our nation's core industries need geopolitical security. We provide great jobs."

—Pat Hassey

"You have to have a *noble* purpose. Toys and material things are not an adequate purpose. It's *not* 'The one who ends up with most toys who wins.'"

—Howard Lance

Thanks

I'm humbled that I'm allowed to be an author of books and a business storyteller who hopefully helps businesspeople achieve their full economic potential. I always look forward to a book's completion and being able to thank everyone who helped me with the project.

The Publishing Team

It's been my ambition to complete a new business book every two years but the sheer volume of numbers crunching and field research required for this book took an extra year. Special thanks to my publisher Adrian Zackheim and his team at Portfolio for their constant encouragement and understanding. Adrian's patient guidance and support won't be forgotten. Adrienne Schultz served as the book's editor and her advice and guidance were terrific. She's a tough taskmaster and made me work harder than any previous editor. But as she says, "Hard work never killed anyone." Special thanks also to Cynthia Baskin, who copyedited the book and made it easier for you to read. Allison McLean handles promotion and publicity for Portfolio and is the best in the business. Special thanks also to Will Weisser, the head of marketing for Portfolio, who always looks out for the best interests of my books. And to Mark Fortier Public Relations in New York, a welcome addition to the team.

Thanks to my literary agent, Alan Nevins of The Firm Entertainment, Beverly Hills, California.

My Right Arms

Caryn Shehi is my personal assistant and the person responsible for booking my speeches, coordinating my travel, maintaining my calendar, and keeping my life running smoothly. She does all that superbly and a whole lot more. Christopher DiSalvio, my bookkeeper and financial assistant, handles all financial chores. Mark Powell, of Casto Travel, books the travel and figures out how to get me from one place to another, and drivers Wit, Steve, and Reuben coordinated by Nadia make sure I show up where I'm supposed to be. Marc Moellinger is our Web master and does a superb job of keeping everyone connected with readers. It would be impossible to write a book like this without the Internet. Bill Deane, Kori Harvala, and Brett Hanson make sure we all stay connected.

The Research Team

My special thanks go out to everyone who assisted me with the research for this book (see Research section). They include Dr. Carlos Baradello, associate dean of the business school at the University of San Francisco, who helped me assemble a research team composed of brilliant MBA students; Grace Tan, the research team's leader; and team members Vivek Sriram, Steve Epstein, and Jennifer Colvin.

Laurence Haughton, my coauthor on *It's Not the Big That Eat the Small . . . It's the Fast That Eat the Slow,* joined me as a collaborator during the field research and writing. The book is infinitely better because of his keen intellect and skill set.

The Word Gallery in Corte Madera, California, handled the

thousands of pages of interview transcripts quickly and flawlessly as always.

The CEOs, Their Communications Directors, and Their Assistants

Working with the CEOs was one of the greatest business pleasures I've known. They are each the best at what they do.

The VPs of communication and communications directors of the companies distinguished themselves by being the most helpful and proficient professionals with whom I've ever associated. They include Dan Greenfield of Allegheny Technologies, Jim Burke of Harris Corporation, Tom Noland of Humana, Robert Webb of Mohawk Industries, Chad Jones of Questar, Lisa Bottle of Goodrich Corporation, Michael Buckley of The Hanover Group, Maribeth Badertscher of J. M. Smucker, and Paul Capelli of Staples.

The Promotional Team

Pam Lontos and her team at PR/PR in Orlando, Florida, always do a great job with the promotion of my books.

Speaking Agencies

All my speeches are booked through speakers' agencies. If I listed a few of them here, I'd risk offending those I failed to mention and perhaps lose business, so I'll refrain. But I wouldn't be able to do eighty speeches annually around the world without the help of these highly skilled and talented people.

Family and Personal Team

I'm grateful to my family for truly understanding the nature of my work and for their patience and complete support. In addition to family, there's another group of people who keep me healthy, grounded, and centered.

Jeff Marth is my trainer in the gym, Zamil Sadiq is my viola teacher, and Ana Baradello my Spanish tutor. Each is relentless in working me hard, but they've all become close friends and big boosters of my work. Not a workout or lesson goes by without each of them asking questions about my research and writing.

When we designed Timber Rock Shores, our family lodge on the shores of a small lake in the wilderness of Michigan's remote Upper Peninsula, we hoped it would become a peaceful retreat for writing, relaxation, and creative expression. Through the efforts of Gene and Judy Nagle, who take care of it (and us when we're there), it's become all we dreamed it would be.

You

Thanks for purchasing and reading *Hit the Ground Running*. Please recommend it to others because that's the way successful books happen. I hope you'll also consider reading my previous books from the Portfolio imprint of Penguin, including *Less Is More* and *Think Big, Act Small*.

If you happen to attend one of my speeches, please take the time to introduce yourself and say hello. I truly enjoy spending time with readers. If you'd like to contact me, please visit our Web site at www .jason-jennings.com, click "contact us," and send an e-mail. I try to respond to all e-mails. My only request is that you don't send me any ideas for future books. My research and publishing journey is an intensely private and personal one and the ideas and words need to be mine.

I hope to be back very soon with another book filled with more stories of great businesspeople and how they and their companies are achieving their full economic potential.

The Research

The original research team for *Hit the Ground Running* comprised MBA students from the University of San Francisco (USF). Midway through the project I was joined by Laurence Haughton, who has been my business colleague for twenty years and who spearheaded gaining access to the CEOs, serving as an invaluable sounding board, font of great ideas, and writing assistant.

Phase I: Deciding Who We'd Study

The first task of the research team was to decide how to define a "best performing" CEO. Rather than start with a CEO's reputation, values, or strategies, we decided to start with performance metrics that we could prove. Our choice to use stock price as an objective way of comparing CEO performance among companies was based on a belief that the market is fair. Regardless of what happens in the short term, a company's stock price in the long run will reflect its true value. And since stock prices reflect a variety of other factors, including debt loads, stock splits, and dividends, it was clear that stock price was the best single metric we could use.

To determine which CEOs had created the most shareholder value in the first few years of their tenure, our research relied on publicly available financial data. Because of this constraint, we ruled out privately owned companies since they aren't required to make their financial statements public.

The *Fortune* 1000 seemed a reasonable place to start, but that didn't narrow it sufficiently. We wondered how far back we should go to analyze CEO performance. We considered looking at CEOs who had started as long as fifteen years ago, and as recently as two and a half years ago. Recognizing that many factors outside a new CEO's control could influence a company's stock price shortly after the transition (such as consequences of decisions made by the previous CEO and the stock market response to a change in leadership), we set two and a half years as the minimum tenure for a CEO to ensure that he or she had been in the leadership role long enough to have a significant impact on the company. When we started to dig into the research, we quickly determined that going back fifteen years was going to yield a lot of out-of-date information. CEO turnover in the *Fortune* 1000 has reached record levels in recent years, with 47 percent of the companies in the *Fortune* 1000 changing CEOs.

We decided the best lessons could be learned from new CEOs who created the most shareholder value in recent years despite the challenges posed by the stock market crash in 2000, the terrorist attacks of 2001, and the passage of the Sarbanes-Oxley accounting reform law in 2002. So we set out to identify the CEOs for *Fortune* 1000 companies who started their tenure between January 1, 2000, and January 1, 2004, and who had served at least two and a half years.

Digging through news databases and company Web sites, we found 370 CEOs in the *Fortune* 1000 who fit the criteria. Our next step was to narrow the list even further. We eliminated CEOs who were not currently with their companies and those who didn't have valid stock data due to bankruptcy or mergers. That left us with 265 companies for Phase II of the research.

Phase II: Analyzing Financial Performance

Using Yahoo! Finance, Bloomberg, Hoovers, and the *Wall Street Journal* as our primary sources of stock data, we calculated the percentage change in the adjusted daily closing price of each company's stock, beginning six months prior to the change in CEO up to three years into the CEO's tenure, or by June 2007, whichever was earlier. By using the stock price six months prior to the new CEO's start date, we could eliminate the consequences of any fluctuations in stock price that might have occurred immediately before the transition to new leadership. And by limiting the length of the comparison to three years (or by June 2007), we could ensure a fair comparison over a similar period of time for each company.

That left us with 207 companies that had a positive change in stock price over the first three years of the CEO's tenure. The increase in stock price ranged from a measly 0.2 percent to a whopping 1,800 percent, with an average increase of 109 percent. Reasoning that any CEO who had led a company with a 100 percent increase in stock price over the first three years of his or her tenure was worth further investigation, we set that amount as the cutoff for the next phase of research. We were left with 56 companies.

Phase III: Digging Deeper

Next, we began building dossiers on each of the companies consisting of hundreds of pages of research on their products and services, history, competitors, executives, lawsuits, and current news. We scoured newspapers, magazines, industry publications, analyst reports, and blogs, and we searched company Web sites, press releases, and annual reports. With all this information together in once place, we began to develop a better understanding of the factors that contributed to each company's past successes and to identify some red flags that called into question their potential success in the future.

Based on this research, we ranked the companies and identified the most obvious ones for exclusion; some had several class action lawsuits filed against them, others were irresponsible corporate citizens, and one even had an entire MSN Group dedicated to its negative press. Our decisions would have to pass the scrutiny of a group of advisers that included Carlos Baradello, associate dean and professor at the University of San Francisco's graduate school of management and venture capitalist; Bruce Ritter, a financial counselor based in San Rafael, California; and Mark Thompson, an executive coach and coauthor of *Success Built to Last*.

While we were able to eliminate twenty-three companies, we realized we had more research to do before we could narrow the list down even further. Bruce Ritter pointed out the value of comparing the remaining companies on our list with their competitors and factoring in other performance measures such as earnings per share (EPS) and earnings before interest, taxes, depreciation, and amortization (EBITDA) before making any further decisions. We went back to the financial numbers.

Phase IV: Verifying All Previous Research

Soon after we began to compare the remaining thirty-three companies with their competitors, a couple of companies emerged that had qualified but hadn't made it on our original Phase III list. An error in an earlier spreadsheet was identified, and we immediately set out to verify the accuracy of all previous research and identified an additional nine companies that had a 100 percent or greater increase in stock price over the first three years of their current CEO's tenure.

We were left with forty-seven companies that needed to be compared against other companies in the same *Fortune* 1000 industry that had increases in their share prices.

Phase V: Comparing Companies with Their Competitors

We sorted the 47 companies into 27 industries. Using the results from Phase II of the research, we identified all companies in the same industry that had an increase in share price of any amount during the CEO's first three years. That left us with 124 companies for further financial analysis. After calculating EPS and EBITDA for all 124 companies beginning two quarters before the current CEO's start date through three years after, we had a more complete picture of each company's financial performance in comparison to its peers.

Through this extra level of analysis we discovered two additional companies that hadn't passed our initial screening but clearly had strong numbers in these other areas and were added to the list. With the EPS and EBITDA numbers, we were also able to eliminate fourteen of the forty-seven companies that had 100 percent or more increases in stock price but whose other financial numbers were negative or less than stellar.

Left with thirty-three companies in twenty-two industries, the team began to take a hard look at the industries themselves. Because the last thing we wanted was to include companies in declining industries, we eventually eliminated homebuilding, wholesale electronics, and mining companies (because of the repeated guilty verdicts for polluting the environment against the two mining companies that had surfaced during the research).

Finally, we were left with 12 companies that had survived each phase of research and scrutiny. We were ready to start the interviews.

Phase VI: Interviewing the CEOs

Laurence Haughton directed the effort that resulted in our gaining access to the CEOs of the companies. This was a difficult task. My earlier books were about companies, not the people who head them, and gaining access was easier. For this book, we had to be up front in stating that this book was about the people who head the companies and that our primary focus would be on the CEO. Haughton's middle name should be "perseverance" because he was eventually successful in gaining access to a group of people who were hesitant to talk about themselves.

I conducted the interviews with the CEOs and all interviews were recorded and transcribed. For some interviews I traveled solo; on other occasions I was joined by Steve Epstein or Laurence Haughton.

Phase VI: The Writing

As chapters were completed, they were submitted to the respective company for fact checking and accuracy. They were *not* allowed to approve either the chapter's narrative or its conclusions.

Members of the Team

Laurence Haughton has spent twenty years researching and explaining successful strategies for fast and flawless leadership in business.

In 1999 Haughton traveled the globe with me, studying the fastest companies for *It's Not the Big That Eat the Small . . . It's the Fast That Eat the Slow.* The book was on the *Wall Street Journal, USA Today,* and the *New York Times* bestseller lists. Published in thirty-two languages, the book was named by *USA Today* as one of the top twenty-five books of 2001.

Next, Haughton analyzed why half of all the best-laid plans in business fail and what leaders could do to start executing flawlessly for his next book, *It's Not What You Say . . . It's What You Do.*

Haughton has interviewed over five thousand entrepreneurs and executives in his career as a business writer, producer, journalist, and management consultant. But more important than the depth of his expertise is that Haughton tells great stories that make it easy for everyone to get the point.

Laurence Haughton has created and led workshops for technology, media, insurance services, manufacturing, and retail companies as well as trade associations, leadership forums, and event companies.

Prior to publication of that breakthrough book on speed, Haughton traveled the United States and Asia for fifteen years as the chief strategist for my consulting company, working with media companies, retail and distribution businesses, service providers, and manufacturers.

Grace Tan was a Dean's Fellow at the University of San Francisco, where she served as the program coordinator of the nationwide top-tier USF Entrepreneurship Program. She graduated with an MBA in marketing and entrepreneurship (summa cum laude) in 2007. Prior to that, Grace led the marketing department of her family business in Singapore. Grace was selected by the research team to serve as the lead research associate during the quantitative research process.

Jennifer Colvin has ten years of marketing experience with organizations as varied as REI and Microsoft. She has a passion for finding ways to help organizations achieve their goals by conveying the essence of their brands to customers, employees, and others. She received her MBA in marketing from USF in 2007.

Steve Epstein earned degrees in advertising and education and a MBA from USF, where he received the Dean's Service Award for outstanding service to the school of business and management and to university life. His experience has included sales, teaching, and educational nonprofit management.

Vivek Sriram earned his MBA from USF. He is director of partner services at Aggregate Knowledge, a start-up Web services software company specializing in behavioral personalization, where he is responsible for managing customer relationships.

Our Advisory Committee

The following people served on our advisory committee and helped establish the guidelines for quantitatively identifying and vetting the companies studied:

Dr. Carlos Baradello combines unique business and academic credentials as an entrepreneurial senior technology executive with hands-on experience in the U.S. and global markets, including Europe and Latin America. He is cofounder and general partner of the Sienna Hispanic Fund based in Sausalito, California. Carlos teaches at the School of Business and Management, University of San Francisco, and the School of Business & Economics at Saint Mary's College in the areas of globalization, risks and opportunities of a networked world, global new product development, wireless telecommunications, social entrepreneurship, and the growing importance of the U.S. Hispanic market and the role in the economic development and integration of the Americas. Carlos's academic background includes an electrical-electronic engineering degree from the Universidad Católica de Córdoba, Argentina, a master's degree in electronic engineering from Eindhoven International Institute of the Eindhoven University of Technology in the Netherlands and a Ph.D. in electrical engineering from Carnegie Mellon University in the United States.

Mark Thompson is one of America's top executive coaches and has interviewed hundreds of the world's enduringly successful people, from presidents of nations, billionaires, and Olympians to Academy Award winners, Nobel Laureates, and CEOs.

The coauthor of the international bestseller *Success Built to Last,* he has two decades of experience as a senior executive, board member, management coach, producer, and investor in growing businesses. He is also the author of many audio and video programs, including the *Charles Schwab CEO* series, *Women on Leadership, Seven Sacred Secrets* with Maya Angelou, and the DVD program *Creating a Life That Matters.*

Mark is a former member of the board of Best Buy Enterprises, Korn Ferry International, Interwoven, and Teletech. He served on the board of the National Investor Relations Institute and Seniornet .com and the U.S. SEC Consumer Advisory Council.

Bruce Ritter is an investment adviser who serves a clientele of high net worth individuals and professional athletes. A U.S. Securities and Exchange Commission registered investment adviser, he has been ranked by Bloomberg's *Wealth Manager* magazine as one of America's top seventy-five wealth managers annually since 2003.

He received a bachelor of science in business management from Montana State University in 1981. He owned and managed his own retail clothing business from 1982 to 1985. In 1986, he received an MBA in financial planning from Golden Gate University. Mr. Ritter has taught personal financial planning to employees of several corporations and does personal finance education for professional athletes as well as student-athletes of all ages.

Mr. Ritter is a National Football League Players' Association registered financial adviser. He is a member of the Sports Financial Advisors Association, the Wealth Advisor Institute, and an associate member for the Sports Lawyers Association.

Index

Index

Index

Index